BE HEALTHY

What does being healthy mean to you?

The first thing that might come to mind is the body. But there's something just as important that is often overlooked – your mental health. Being healthy is about tuning into what your body and mind need to work together harmoniously. Would 10 minutes of yoga help you to feel calm and energised? What about going for a sunset stroll? Could a citrus smoothie give your brain a boost before that exam?

A positive relationship between body and mind can give you greater energy, a more resilient immune system and strength to cope with life's stresses. Eating well, exercising, connecting with others, getting creative and taking time to reflect – all of these things require some level of effort, but if you can find the right way to embrace them, none of them have to be hard work.

So, whether you want to learn how to break bad habits, put a stop to negative thoughts or simply get more active, this book is for you. We hope you discover something you'd never thought of before when it comes to taking care of your health.

LEARN TO THRIVE

CONTENTS

HAPPY AND HEALTHY

Being healthy isn't just about looking after your body – it's about nurturing your mind, too. Here are 10 ways you can feel happy and healthy in both...

1 Develop good habits
Being healthier in body and mind doesn't have to come down to sheer willpower, it's about developing new habits – you don't need to decide to try and get up at 6am if it's something you do automatically. If you've developed a bad habit, think about why you do it – what you get from it – and what you could do instead that will give you the same reward. Maybe you reach for a chocolate bar every evening as a way to escape your busy day. Going for a run, reading a book, listening to a podcast – what could give you the same comfort?

2 Be mindful
Take time each day to appreciate the world around you, understand your body and just 'be'. Start small – it can be any mundane activity you perform every day, like washing your hands. Instead of rushing through it, slow down and give the task your full attention. Try some yoga poses to help you get in tune with your body.

3 Exercise

Staying active is at the core of every healthy person's routine. We're not saying you have to run 10 kilometres every day before school – there's plenty of small ways you can stay fit and keep healthy. Changing the type of exercise you do every day can make things more fun – for example, one day yoga, the next day a team sport, another day go for a walk.

4 Let go of perfect

Unrealistic expectations of yourself can lead to worrying, and the problem with perfectionism is that it doesn't allow you to make mistakes and learn from them. So readjust your thinking. If a friendship, relationship or school project is mostly right, then you're doing well. Those times when you stumble can be stepping stones and failure can teach you valuable lessons. Worried that you've failed at something in the past? Adopt a fresh attitude and realise that doesn't mean you'll never succeed. Failure is part of the process. Remember this quote from basketball player Michael Jordan: 'I've missed more than 9,000 shots in my career. I've failed over and over and over again in my life. And that is why I succeed.'

5 Inhale fresh air

Get outside! Don't be sofa-shaped, instead absorb some daylight and all-important vitamin D, and get a dose of nature too. Being out in the fresh air means you'll not only be getting a little exercise, but it's proven to be fantastic for unburdening the mind. You could take a short walk in the park, meditate in your back garden or dip your toes in the sea. Whatever you choose, take it as a chance to unplug, leave your phone at home and have a break from technology.

6 Be kind

Help yourself by helping others. Research shows that doing something for other people can lead to greater happiness, fewer worries and better overall health. Small acts of kindness can be just as important as volunteering your time – hold the door open for someone, bake an elderly neighbour some cookies, call a friend to check how they are.

7 Get more sleep

Sleep is essential; it allows the body to rejuvenate and the mind to rest. A regular routine is the most important thing, so try to get to bed at the same time each night and you'll figure out the amount of sleep that is right for you. And switch off your phone an hour before bed – the blue light from smartphones overstimulates your brain. It's all about creating the right conditions for your body to feel relaxed.

8 Take time out

Learn to listen to your body. Get to know the signs your body gives you – from this you can better understand its needs. Rest when you need to, eat regularly and avoid putting your body under unnecessary stress. Make a point of setting aside time for a night in or some time out just for you.

9 Eat well

What you choose to fuel your body with is the root of any healthy routine – the secret isn't dieting, it's eating sensibly. The food you eat has a direct impact on mood and endorphin levels, so stick to the good stuff – dark leafy greens, berries, nuts and seeds, yoghurts, dark chocolate. Taking time to learn to cook is an easy way to control what goes into your meals and needn't be the chore it sounds. In fact, it's more about getting into a routine than anything else. Get organised and you'll find adopting a healthy lifestyle much easier.

10 Smile

It's a fact – smiling and laughing releases the endorphin serotonin into the body, which makes you feel fantastic and is physically good for you too. Not only is smiling great for your mental health, it reduces stress, and can even improve your health at a cellular level. Research from biochemist Sondra Bennet suggests that smiling will help your cells release tension, which can help you fight off illness. So show off those pearly whites whenever you can!

OUT OF HABIT

Changing everyday habits that impact life for better or worse is not easy but there are ways to build healthier routines that stick around

Do you often try to kick habits you know aren't good for you – only to run out of steam and return to your normal routine a few days later? So many of us begin plans with optimism, only to find sticking to them trickier than we thought. But why are old habits so tough to kick? And why is it so hard to form new ones? Several factors work against us, but with increased awareness, we can become creatures of new, different habits. The dictionary defines habits as automatic behaviours done repeatedly on a regular basis. They are formed gradually and become second nature, allowing you to work on autopilot as you perform them without really thinking. Some habits are positive, such as practising an instrument for two hours every day to improve your playing. The issue comes from habits developed unintentionally that can have a negative impact, for example, eating unhealthy food all the time or sitting badly at your desk.

According to researchers at Duke University in North Carolina, habits account for around 45 per cent of everyday behaviours. And while changing them may seem difficult, it's not impossible. First, though, we need a greater understanding of how habits are developed and a clever approach to shaking them off.

How are habits formed?

Habit formation involves three parts: trigger, action and reward. The trigger is an event that begins the action, the action is the behaviour itself and the reward is the benefit you get from performing the action.

Probably one of the first things you do in the morning is brush your teeth. You don't have to remember to do this, it's automatic. In this case, the trigger is waking up, the action is brushing your teeth and the reward is fresh, minty breath. The ultimate secret to building long-lasting healthy habits is the emotional reward the body gets from carrying out the action, because this is what drives the three-part habit loop and makes you do things without the need for willpower. Repetition of the three-part loop will result in the brain remembering the context of the habit – but it takes a while for this to happen.

Habits take time to break – and patience to form.

HOW TO BUILD NEW ROUTINES

When it comes to making things happen, we often want to see quick results, but the truth is you need consistency, sustained motivation and persistence. Remember Aesop's fable *The Tortoise and the Hare*? Slow and steady wins the race.

Take the following small steps now to reap rewards sooner rather than later:

1 Practise mindfulness
The practice of mindfulness offers the ability to pause and consciously recognise and reflect on actions and reactions. In this way, you can become aware of how involuntary habits have a powerful effect and assess whether they are positive or negative and if you want to keep or lose them, be it changing what you eat or sitting up straight at your desk. Be mindful as you go about your day and become aware of all your habits. If you find it hard to notice the less great ones, be brave and ask someone close to you. Now pick a negative action from your list – the one you would most like to change. This is the first bad habit you are going to work on replacing with a healthier alternative.

2 Develop a strategy
Write down the bad habit you have chosen including the trigger, action and reward. Then note down the action and reward of the good habit you would like to replace it with. When choosing the new habit, make sure it's really rewarding – it needs to evoke an emotion in you. For example, if you choose to sit up straight and improve your posture at your desk, allow yourself an extra 10 minutes of screen time as a reward. This will stimulate the release of feel-good chemicals in your brain, helping you to wire the habit much quicker and make it stick.

3 Value versus cost
To break a bad habit and form a new one, you need to have a strong enough reason to make it happen. Ask yourself how the new habit will improve your life. It will give you a sense of urgency as you realise it needs to change now, not tomorrow or the day after.

4 Mental rehearsal

Free your mind of distractions and focus on a mental picture of the situation you will be in when you are going to form the habit. Think about what you will see, hear, feel, touch and smell. Imagine the trigger happening and, as a result, actively following through on the action. Having done this, imagine the rush of positive feelings that flood your senses. Now open your eyes. Take a moment to consider how you will feel in a week's time if you stick to your habit. Then it's time to start doing it in real life.

5 Take action

Keep repeating the three-part loop over days or weeks until it becomes wired into your brain. It's easy to have a momentary relapse into an old habit. Should this happen, don't get down on yourself or let it stop you in your tracks. Just keep remembering why forming the new habit is important.

6 Time to reflect

Plan time out every week to reflect on the progress you have made with your habit. Make sure there's a trigger to remind you. For example, you could choose Sunday morning after breakfast. Think about your progress in the week, the challenges you encountered, and how you overcame them. Jot down your thoughts, so you can keep track and refer back to them if necessary.

7 Call for backup

Get one of your family members or friends to be your backup or support partner – someone who you can turn to for support and will check up to see how you're doing. To motivate you even more, come up with a consequence if you don't follow through on your action daily, such as cleaning your mum's car if she's your backup partner. Also think of a treat for when you do complete your new habits regularly.

Old habits can hold you back. Embracing new ones can change your life – and by changing your life you can fulfil your potential.

BLAME MY BRAIN

Feeling uncharacteristically moody and lazy? Or being unusually careless and unreasonable? Don't worry, science says this is a normal reflection of the changes going on in your head

It's all in your head

The brain has a lot to answer for, most of which is all good and A-OK. Between the ages of about 12 and 25, however, it undergoes significant changes that affect emotions, thinking and learning. It craves stimulation and novelty, is eager to learn new experiences (really quickly) and it isn't afraid to take risks during this process of development. It encourages you to explore further and face new challenges (and errors) every day. But this drive to learn also brings with it confusion and uncertainty. It's a tough time, especially when many are struggling to forge an identity that truly reflects who they are. Navigating this journey to adulthood can leave you feeling unstable and vulnerable – and it can affect your personality.

Work in progress

Science has demonstrated there are neurological, biological and sociological reasons for any out-of-character behaviour. Neurologically, the brain is readjusting your reasoning, logic and decision-making, so it isn't surprising if you become more impulsive, unpredictable and irrational while it does this. It all makes sense now. Losing self-control? Bound to. Enjoying taking risks? Inevitable. Angry at the world (and yourself)? All normal. It's hard to adapt to the ups and downs and the many new complex situations, intense emotions, unexpected freedoms (and unfair limitations) – and to the new 'you' in progress. Neuroscientist Frances E Jensen compares the teenage brain to a shiny new car that you struggle to control: 'The brain just doesn't know how to regulate itself yet. They're like Ferraris with weak brakes. It's revved up, but doesn't always know how to stop.' Like a car, then, with guidance, practice and perseverance comes control.

Unlock your inner power

Your brain can be blamed for many things, but try not to use it as an excuse or get-out clause. You could think of it as a supercomputer – hugely complex with extraordinary powers – and yourself as the programmer, on a mission to teach it to make sensible choices and to deal with difficult emotions (embarrassment, anger) and handle stressful situations (exams, public speaking). Science has shown that your brain doesn't control you – the opposite is the case. You can learn to control it. Training the brain to 'behave itself' is like exercising any muscle, but it takes mental rather than physical strength. Brain exercise can improve memory and focus, boost the ability to stay calm under pressure and even encourage feelings of happiness.

A balanced mind

Of course, learning to control your brain isn't easy. It takes effort and practice but the opportunity is there for everyone. It involves working hard enough to find out how you personally can be more positive, energised and productive to improve your quality of life. The upshot? Yes, the changes going on in your brain right now are causing you some short-term hiccups. But rather than blaming it for everything, try to see the brain as the most powerful tool you possess – the key that will allow you to unlock and maximise your potential. Still, it's all well and good to build mental strength and endurance... but how do you do that? There are a few strategies, which, taken together, can help to manage difficult emotions and enable you to think more clearly. Turn the page to discover how to unlock your brain and reach your inner 'ninja mind'.

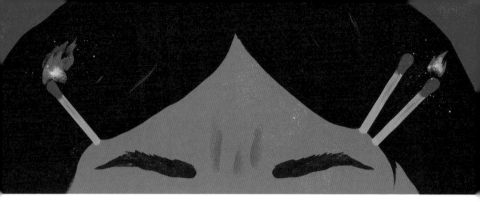

HOW TO RE-TRAIN YOUR BRAIN

Exercise – *for energy*
As well as the physical benefits, exercising also brings a great mental boost. It increases brain power by improving mood and reducing stress, making you feel more energetic and helping you to sleep better. It makes your brain work better: physical activity burns cortisol, the hormone produced by the body under stress, and releases happy hormones, endorphin and serotonin. Just a walk around your local park or a dance in your bedroom will work wonders for body and brain.

Be positive – *for happiness*
The brain is wired to focus on all the bad things that happen and sometimes small negatives can become bigger and bigger to the point where you see only doom and gloom. Try to remember that the world isn't as bad as your brain suggests. You can break the cycle and even reverse it. Ways to do this include not comparing yourself to others, making a note of all your achievements and focusing on the many positives in your life no matter how small they might appear. Added up, they grow into a positive energy that floods your brain with those feel-good endorphins. Repetition creates new habits, and with time and practice, you can rewire your brain to automatically make you see life in a brighter (and better) light.

Reveal yourself – *for authenticity*
In the heat of the moment, your inner negative voice may get to you, overwhelming you with fear, jealousy or anger. Intense emotions are natural. The important thing is how you manage them, and expressing how you really feel will help to release any emotional pressure. One solution is to write or draw your emotions in a journal, while another might be to talk to someone who won't judge you. Your aim is to identify difficult situations and think them through in a constructive way.

Sleep better – *for productivity*

Sleep, like exercise, is food for a healthy brain. Lack of sleep is one of the main contributors to anxiety problems. If you haven't had enough sleep, you may feel moody and find it harder to take in new thoughts and concentrate. Experts suggest that young adults need between eight and 10 hours of sleep each night to function effectively. If you're feeling more grouchy than usual, think about looking at your sleeping pattern. Are you staying up too late on school nights? Is your sleep being disrupted by the constant pinging of notifications on your phone? Try to improve your sleeping habits by establishing a night-time routine (think about turning off your phone an hour before you sleep) so that you're more likely to wake feeling rested and ready to face another eventful day.

Be cautious – *for wisdom*

Each day brings new temptations. When your brain says 'go, go, go!', stop and think for a second. You may feel invincible – the impulsive side of your brain is pretty much in charge and you'll feel like breaking the rules and being as reckless as some of your peers. But be warned. Rules (mostly) exist for a reason and other students sometimes do dumb things, so always think before you act.

FIT FOR LIFE

Too fat, too thin, too tall, too short. Most people have hang-ups that put them off taking part in sports. Yet physical activity is one of the best ways to keep your body and mind healthy – now and in the future

Guess what... you've won the evolutionary lottery. You are the lucky owner of the most evolved biological system on planet Earth – your amazing body, human brain and nervous system. But when do you ever feel like that? It's a bit like owning a Ferrari and never knowing it can shift up from first gear. Yet women of all ages have proven they have – and know how to use – top gear. At the 2019 Wimbledon tennis championship, 15-year-old Coco Gauff became the youngest player to qualify for the main draw in the tournament's history, reaching the fourth round of the event.

For many, however, real worries about body image, the thought of a red face, sweating too much, and a general feeling of clumsiness or being judged make sport a no-go area. Uninspiring PE programmes don't help either – 51 per cent of less-active girls say gym classes and sports at school actually put them off being physically active – and the fear of just not being very good is a common anxiety.

Sport for wellbeing

Physical activity isn't just about being fit. It promotes a positive outlook and emotional intelligence because it has a deep and long-lasting impact on wellbeing. How? It's all down to mood-enhancing endorphins that are produced by the brain during exercise. At the same time, the stress hormone cortisol is lowered, so you are less likely to feel anxious. Exercise really can lift your mood like nothing else.

Here are just a few of the benefits of regular exercise:

* Healthy bones and muscles.
* Positive mental wellbeing and reduced feelings of depression and anxiety.
* Better cognitive function and improved self-confidence.
* Improved sleep.
* A broad social network.
* Good team-building skills and a sense of community (witness the 2019 World Cup triumph of the US women's football team).
* A place to find your voice and reach out to positive role models who truly reflect your values and feed your mind and self-image with good vibes only.
* It can keep you fit and switched on throughout life.

So, as hard as it might be, try to stop worrying about how you look (there are few people of any age who feel totally confident about their body) because sport could support you when you need it the most. Health and fitness matter more than looks and size. Physical activity will help you to feel calmer, less anxious and more aware of your inner feelings – and more able to perform at crucial events, both on and off the pitch. From competitive races to exams and interviews to stage acting, the wellbeing benefits of exercise can help you get to the starting line like a champion.

This girl can

Just like an elite athlete at the starting line you, too, can experience the many wellbeing benefits of sport and fitness.

   This Girl Can is a campaign celebrating active women who are doing their thing no matter how they look, how red their face gets or how 'well' they do it. It aims to help women overcome the fear of judgment that stop so many from even thinking about trying sports they might love. Find out more at thisgirlcan.co.uk.

FIND YOUR SPORT

From running to rowing and boxing to badminton, there's a sport out there with your name on it. The important thing is to find an activity you enjoy. There are many clubs around the country where you can cycle, swim, play hockey, netball or soccer, practise yoga or perform gymnastics – an online search will identify the ones closest to you. In the meantime, here are a few less obvious possibilities:

Pickleball. Part badminton, part tennis. This is one of the fastest-growing games in the UK. Learn more at pickleballportal.com.

Roller derby. An adrenaline-fuelled, full-contact game, where players skate around an elliptical track trying to block opponents. Sign up at UKRDA.org.uk.

Indoor climbing. An increasingly popular sport that improves fitness and coordination. Many clubs run taster sessions, which are a great way to start out. Visit the British Mountaineering Council at thebmc.co.uk for details.

Let's dance. Recent research has shown that dance comes only second to football as the most popular activity of choice for high-school age students. Search online for classes and groups in your area or try danceschools-uk.co.uk as a starting point.

SET TO CHANGE

Your attitude towards life – sometimes called a mindset – can affect your overall sense of wellbeing. It determines whether you see things as problems or challenges, and view mistakes as setbacks or opportunities. Luckily, mindsets are changeable. And learning how to adopt one that encourages growth could bring fresh openings and possibilities

Do you ever find yourself saying or thinking statements such as: 'I'm stupid', 'I'm terrible at spelling', 'I'm good at maths', 'I'm not a creative person' or 'I'll never be able to make friends'. Many people believe intelligence, abilities and other personal characteristics are things they're born with – and that they will stay the same way for life. In reality, individual traits and abilities aren't fixed. All these things change and become stronger or weaker over time, depending on how much effort and practice a person puts in. The brain is like any other muscle in the body – it grows stronger with use. Learning something new or practising a skill means certain neurons (cells that communicate with each other in the brain) are used more. These new connections are then strengthened. Things you might once have found hard – doing algebra, riding a bike or speaking another language, for example – become easier and require less effort. You literally have changed how your brain works.

Fixed mindset

Unfortunately, many people miss out on growing their brain because they have a fixed mindset – they're convinced they'll never be able to change. They stick with what they know they can do and steer clear of challenges.

They also tend to give up early on and think things like: 'I won't be able to do that' or 'I don't want to fail'. Individuals with a fixed mindset avoid things they find difficult. They might also believe they don't need to keep practising at subjects they're already good at.

Growth mindset

Other people have what's called a growth mindset. They believe they can learn, change and develop new skills. Individuals who choose a growth mindset are inclined to thrive on challenges. They don't see mistakes as failure but as an opportunity to learn and improve. Research shows those with a growth mindset are more persistent and better equipped to deal with setbacks – they know hard work and practice can help them to reach their goals.

You could be... anything

You can have a fixed mindset in some situations ('I'm bad at making new friends') and a growth mindset in other areas ('I'll get better at gymnastics if I continue to train regularly'). It's possible to develop more of a growth mindset in any aspect of life by paying attention to your thoughts and attitudes in different circumstances. Having a growth mindset isn't about unrealistically believing that you'll become the next Stephen Hawking and unravel the mysteries of the universe nor is it comparing your achievements to those of others. In a growth mindset the person believes they have the capability to change and improve at their own pace. A growth mindset leaves open the possibility that things might be different from what you expect. You approach new experiences with curiosity rather than fixed ideas and thoughts about how you'll do. By viewing life with a growth mindset you come to see your potential is unknown – and there are heaps of things you'll achieve with ongoing passion, effort and a positive attitude.

SWITCHING MINDSET

Do you ever find yourself in a fixed mindset?

* I'm no good at...
* I think I'll never get better at...
* Sometimes I avoid... because I think I'll fail.

Change your fixed mindset thoughts into growth mindset thoughts:

* 'This is too hard' **becomes** 'This might take more time and effort than I expected'.
* 'I won't be able to do this so I won't bother trying' **becomes** 'I like a challenge. It's worth a try'.
* 'I give up' **becomes** 'I'll try out some of the strategies I've learnt'.
* 'I'm brilliant at history' **becomes** 'I still need to put effort in to continue to do well at history'.
* 'I've failed' **becomes** 'This mistake will help me to improve next time'.
* 'I'll never be able to make friends' **becomes** 'I'm getting better at making friends all the time'.
* 'I can't speak French' **becomes** 'I'm still learning how to speak French'.

Think about times you have developed a growth mindset:

* A time I learnt from a mistake was...
* I've been trying hard at...
* I've become more confident at...
* I challenged myself when...

'I CAN ACCEPT FAILURE, EVERYONE FAILS AT SOMETHING. BUT I CAN'T ACCEPT NOT TRYING AGAIN'

Michael Jordan

ADDICTED TO ATTENTION

Everyone wants to be noticed, listened to and understood, but if your desire for attention becomes a craving it may be a sign of a deeper problem

Most people like others to notice them and hardly anyone enjoys being ignored. But when you start to crave attention it can be a sign you're seeking other people's approval and that can come from insecurity. When you feel insecure, you might be overwhelmed with a belief that you're just not good enough, whether it's because of your looks, your abilities or your popularity. Feeling worried about these things can make you want to turn to others for reassurance that you're okay, which is fine, but when it turns into a overriding need, it might be time to share these concerns with someone you trust.

What's an addiction?

People can become addicted to all sorts of things – it could be nicotine in cigarettes; caffeine in tea, coffee or cola; sugar; or even exercise. Addiction means a person has no control over their cravings and it can be physical, psychological or both. Being physically addicted to something means the body actually becomes dependent on it. Psychological addiction is far more common and happens when a craving for something takes control of a person's thoughts and emotions. When you're psychologically addicted to something, you feel overcome by the desire to get it. But just as someone can crave substances, they can also crave attention.

Showing off

The world can seem obsessed with fame and beauty and social media can be used as a way of judging popularity and as a platform to seek instant attention. If you post a picture of yourself on Snapchat or Instagram and receive lots of likes, it can make you feel good about yourself. But that feeling doesn't last long and soon you'll want more. If you don't get as good a response from the next post, it can leave you feeling as though you've somehow failed to impress. It might be worth asking yourself: 'Why am I doing this? Is it purely social? Is it to entertain my friends and family, or is it a way of saying, "Look at me! Aren't I great?"'

Attention seeking

An addiction to attention can cause disruption to your life and create negative feelings. No matter how much attention you get, it will most likely never be enough. You may feel insecure if you walk into a party and no one comes running straight over to you to talk, but that's normal. Most people have to make an effort with others to get their attention, so try to go and speak to people yourself. In the same way, you might start fixating on the number of people who react to your posts on Instagram. But people may miss your posts or might not realise how important it is to you that they react. If you find yourself checking your phone every 10 minutes to see who's responded, it could be that your need for attention is beginning to assume too much importance in your life.

Get real

If this sounds like you, talk it through with someone you trust and who you know will keep your confidence. In practical terms, try to be realistic and wean yourself off social media gradually – that doesn't mean abandoning it all together. To start with, don't post any pictures or updates but just respond to other people's posts. Remember that no matter how impressive someone else's life seems to be, you don't have to compete with them for attention. Okay, so they may look great in staged photographs and appear to be surrounded by lots of friends, but pictures can be misleading. People take hundreds of selfies every day and include random 'others' in their photos just to appear popular. This is no way of measuring how liked someone truly is because it's only about appearance.

Focus on others

The only way to judge how liked you are is to have real friends that you can have fun with and rely on when you need help. Having a thousand friends on Facebook is no substitute for a few close buddies who will support you no matter what you look like or what you achieve in life. Use the energy you put into promoting yourself on social media into helping others, whether it's listening to a friend in crisis or encouraging a shy person to come out of their shell. Ask friends how they are feeling rather than what they think of your latest profile picture. The more attention you give others, the more attention they will give you. Put your efforts into being a kind and thoughtful person that people want to be around and you'll get plenty of attention. And it will be the right kind.

HAVING TROUBLE BELIEVING IN YOURSELF?

Here's some advice to try:

DO
* Surround yourself with people who make you feel good.
* Think positive – remind yourself regularly of all your best qualities.
* Help others whenever you can.
* Do things that you love.
* Try something new as often as possible.

DON'T
* Compare yourself to others.
* Forget to make time for yourself.
* Stop trying – everyone makes mistakes.
* Ignore things that are important to you just to fit in.
* Spend time worrying about how you look.
* Bottle it up inside – share problems with someone special.

NOW THERE'S A THOUGHT...

With so many thoughts running through your mind every day it's not easy to spot the unhelpful ones that need to be challenged. But there are ways to catch them and put them to the test

How many thoughts do you think you have in a day?

A hundred? A thousand?
Actually, the experts say people have about 50,000 to 70,000 thoughts every day. No wonder your mind feels so busy.

A lot of the time, all of that thinking is really helpful – you're able to remember answers for a test, have a conversation with a friend or learn to do something new.

So thinking all the time isn't a bad thing... but sometimes, thoughts can bother you or be upsetting.

For example, you might be worried about how you'll do on a test, or how well you will play in an upcoming game. Your mind might get really busy with thoughts like, 'What if I fail the test? I'm so stupid', or 'I'm not ready for the game. I know I won't do well and everyone will laugh at me.'

All those thoughts can end up making you feel miserable.

HOW TO THINK ABOUT YOUR THOUGHTS

1 The first thing is just to notice that you are thinking. Sometimes people can get so wrapped up in their thoughts that they can't focus on anything else. If you can stop and say, 'Right now, I'm thinking. I'm having the thought that I will fail my test', it's like you've taken a step back from the thought. You're noticing the thought, instead of getting caught up in it.

2 Tell yourself that just because you're thinking something, that doesn't mean it's true. Probably everyone in the world has said to themselves at some point, 'I'm so stupid'. If you pause to notice the thought (like you did in step 1), you might remember the times when you did well on a test, or had a great game. You don't have to believe everything you tell yourself.

3 Once you've noticed your thought, see if you can just watch what happens to it. This might sound a bit tricky, so think of it this way: every single thought you have ever had has eventually gone away, right? Can you try to watch this thought and see when it goes away? A really helpful way to do this is to think of your thoughts as:

* Clouds passing through the sky.
* Boats sailing down a long river.
* Carriages on a train passing by.
* Fish swimming through a pond.

4 As you watch your thoughts passing by, see if you can notice the following about them:

* Are they loud or quiet?
* Are they fast or slow?
* Do they change a lot, or do they stay the same?
* Are they happy or sad?

5 Finally, tell yourself that you don't have to do anything with your thought, just like you don't have to do anything with a cloud passing in the sky. You can notice it, watch it and get curious about it, but you don't have to respond to it. When you can do this, your thoughts lose some of their power to upset you or make you feel bad.

So, next time you have a negative thought, try asking yourself some of these questions:

* Is this thought true? Do I know this for sure?
* I get to choose how I react to things.
  What will I choose?
* Is there a different way to look at this situation?
* Is there another thought I could be thinking right now?
* Am I missing some important information? What don't I know?
* What is good right now?

There are many different ways you can think about your thoughts. Maybe one of these examples makes a lot of sense to you – or maybe you can think of your own way to think about what your thoughts do.

VOICE OF TRUTH

Next time you have a negative thought about yourself or your life that you'd like to let go of, try this exercise. Write down the thought and then immediately underneath it write the real truth of the situation, something you would say to a friend. We've filled in the first one to get you started...

Negative thought: I'm so useless, I'll never be good at anything.
Voice of truth: I did really well for trying. If I keep practising I'm sure I'll get better.

LOOK OUT FOR YOU

Looking after your own physical and emotional needs will put you in a better place to help others

If you've ever listened to a safety briefing on a plane, you may have noticed that the flight attendant instructs passengers, in the case of an emergency, to put their own oxygen masks on first, before helping others. Does this sound selfish, or sensible? The reason this advice is given is because oxygen-deprived passengers will be less capable of giving assistance – so not only are they endangering themselves, but potentially others, too. It's not just in emergencies that this thinking is valuable – it also applies to everyday life. As much as people want to be there for their friends and family, it's not easy to look after others if you're not looking after yourself.

What does looking after yourself entail?

Is it doing whatever you want, whenever you want to do it? Not exactly. There's a difference between self-care and self-indulgence – in fact, self-indulgence is often the exact opposite of being kind to yourself. Imagine, for example, you get a terrible cold before an important hockey game. The impulse might be to burrow under blankets and eat stodgy comfort food – but actually, the kind thing to do for yourself in this situation is to get some fresh air, blast the germs away and eat lots of nourishing fruits and vegetables. Not only will you get better more quickly, but you'll also be in a much stronger position to play your best and support your team members in the game. It's not just for the benefit of others that being kind to yourself matters. It's also important for your own mental health and sense of wellbeing. Sometimes it may even appear that self-care involves hurting someone else's feelings – saying 'no' to a request or declining an invitation, for instance. Yet it may be necessary to make sure you don't have too many commitments.

Being kind to yourself matters for physical wellbeing
Eating good food, drinking enough water, exercising, getting enough sleep: all of these are vital for health, which has a bearing on your mind. The fine line between self-care and self-indulgence is apparent here. After all, indulging your whims might feel kinder to yourself in the short term – like skipping training when you're not in the mood – but actually, the opposite is true. Sometimes the kindest thing you can do for yourself is to do the thing that you don't feel like doing, whether it's getting started on that assignment so you're spared the stress of trying to get it all done at the last minute or choosing an early night over a late film.

Consider how you'd support a friend
Often people tend to be far nicer to others than they are to themselves. The support, encouragement and kindness among friends would, in an ideal situation, be mirrored in the relationship that people have with themselves. Think about what you'd say to a friend in a certain situation – 'don't worry, it will be okay', for example, or 'it wasn't your fault' – and then give that advice to yourself.

This highlights one of the tricky things about kindness, and that's the fact that it's not always about actions, but about words. In terms of kindness to yourself, this can be overlooked. Neglecting your health, for example, might soon be noticed by a friend or adult. But what about the way you speak to yourself in your head?

It's important to practise kindness in terms of an inner voice, telling yourself that 'at least you tried' or 'you did your best' or 'you've got this'. Banish any negative internal noise and tell yourself you're great, just as you'd tell a friend, because how you speak to yourself has a huge effect on your confidence – and this can affect what you achieve (which, in turn, affects your confidence. It's a big loop).

How does this play out in real life? Say you don't do as well as you'd hoped on a test, scoring a 6 rather than a 7. If this happened to a friend, you'd most likely say: 'That was a tough test – you studied really hard and did your best. Getting a 6 is a great result, don't worry.' Or how about if a friend missed a catch in a cricket match? Would you criticise or reassure them? You'd encourage them. And it's these kind, supportive words you need to try to make sure you're saying to yourself as well.

How else can you practise self-care?
Making time for yourself in this busy life is definitely a big one, but how you spend that time also matters. Think about what makes you feel unreservedly good, without guilt: shopping, for example, is fun, but sometimes it comes with a side serving of anxiety about the money that's been spent. Do you love reading? Drawing? Being in nature? Spending time with your grandparents? The things that make you deeply happy are the ones worth prioritising. Sometimes, it's really okay to put yourself first.

LETTING GO OF THE PAST

When something scary or upsetting happens, it can leave you feeling anxious and vulnerable. Here we suggest ways to calm the terror and rediscover your confidence

Most of the time, the world – and those around you – will be safe and function in a predictable way. But there are times where the opposite happens and it can leave you worried that you'll be caught up in a disaster or witness a loved one in distress. It's important to remember that such events are rare. The way in which they're sometimes reported, however, can lead the brain to overestimate how often they happen. Sometimes, it also makes you fearful that you, or a loved one, will be in the middle of a frightening incident. There are things you can do, however, to help you cope with these concerns and to move forward if you've gone through an upsetting experience. Hopefully, these suggestions will go some of the way to helping you to take a brave and bold step out into the world, regain your confidence and keep enjoying the life you were meant to live.

WAYS TO REGAIN YOUR CONFIDENCE

Your response is unique
Each person will have a different reaction after something frightening happens. It depends on age, past experiences and temperament. Common responses can be shock, tears, a state of fearfulness or feeling unable to switch off from what has happened. You might wish to avoid any of the places that remind you of the traumatic event and decline activities you previously enjoyed. Physical responses to such an experience can include shaking, sweating and reliving in your head images of the event. None of these things means there's anything wrong with you. They're all normal responses after a frightening encounter.

Look after your basic needs
The most important thing after a distressing event is to ensure you're in a safe environment where you can eat and sleep. Aim to get back into your normal routine as soon as you can – go to sleep and wake at your regular time, eat at the usual hour and attend school. When it feels right, make time to see friends and take part in things you normally enjoy, whether that's going to the cinema, having a coffee-shop lunch or a Saturday shopping trip. If your world suddenly feels turned upside down, it will help to do things that are comfortable and familiar to you. Know that it really can take time to feel less anxious and don't rush yourself.

Talk when it helps
Let those around you know that you'll open up when you feel ready and that it's not helpful for anyone to try to force you to discuss what happened.

Be careful about what you watch on TV
Repeatedly watching distressing or tragic events on television can be linked to poorer outcomes for wellbeing, so it might help to limit your exposure to such broadcasts and stick to positive viewing.

Focus the mind

Trying to block out or not think about a particularly distressing experience might seem helpful, but it's not always the best coping strategy. That said, you may find there are times when distracting your mind is useful. This could involve getting absorbed in a sport or activity you really enjoy or, if you're feeling overwhelmed, counting backwards from 300.

Write or illustrate the story

A frightening event can also cause memories of the event to become jagged and jumbled up in your mind. To help the brain make sense of what happened, talk or write about the event and go over it again and again. Gillian Colville, a clinical psychologist from St George's Hospital, London, says that using stories can be an excellent way to make sense of events. 'If you make a story about what you went through and write it down, draw it in a picture, or in a series of images like a roll of film, it helps to pack away the memories in the brain and then they [might not] bother you so much.'

Draw strength

It's possible to emerge from the aftermath of a frightening or distressing event even stronger than you were before. People sometimes describe having a greater appreciation of life, stronger relationships and the ability to see fresh possibilities.

Seek further support

After a scary incident, it can feel like you live in a new, changed world that is no longer safe. It doesn't mean these feelings will stay forever. For most people they will ease over time. If you continue to be upset and frightened, try to talk about it to a trusted adult – perhaps your guardian or an older relative, or your doctor or school nurse. If you find it too difficult to talk to someone face to face, there are online options.

Childline provides a 24-hour free and confidential telephone, email and chat service for children and young people on 0800 1111 or childline.org.uk
The National Child Traumatic Stress Network has tip sheets, guides and videos on dealing with a traumatic event. See nctsn.org

RIDING LIFE'S WAVES

As you go through life, the waves go up and down, sometimes they're choppy, sometimes they're calm. A yoga posture for building up core strength within, which will help stay afloat, is *Navasana*, aka Boat pose

This strong pose engages with the core to create both physical and mental strength. It tones stomach muscles, strengthens the lower back and maintains a healthy metabolism. It creates greater mental strength, by showing your ability to conquer tricky situations, resulting in increased confidence, sense of self and a balanced mind.

Here's how to get into the pose:

1. Sit on the floor with your legs straight in front of you and your torso upright and strong. Press your hands to the floor, a little behind your hips with your fingers pointing towards your feet. Sit tall and lean back. Take a few breaths here as you find your point of balance on your sitting bones.
2. On an out breath bend your knees and lift your feet off the floor. Engaging your core and stomach muscles, point your legs and feet up towards the sky at an angle that feels comfortable for you.
3. Keeping your arms straight, stretch them out parallel to the floor, holding them on the outside of your legs with your fingers pointing forwards. Take a few in and out breaths, holding the pose for a few seconds – only as long as you are comfortable to do so.
4. On an out breath, lower your legs to the floor and, on an in breath, sit back upright. Observe the strength within your body and how you are feeling.

Students who have neck injuries, headaches, low blood pressure or any other medical conditions where they have been advised not to engage in such an activity are advised not to practise this posture. It should also be avoided by anyone who is – or thinks they might be – pregnant (we know mums like to try these yoga postures too!).

Younger children should always be supervised.

SPICE UP YOUR LIFE

Spices don't just add flavour, they have tremendous
health-giving properties too

Spices are something you no doubt have in your kitchen, in jars in a rack or in
the food cupboard. People use them primarily to season food but many spices
have antimicrobial properties and have been used in medicine for centuries.

What is a spice?

A spice is a seed, fruit, root, bark, berry, bud or other vegetable substance. It differs from herbs, which are parts of leafy green plants, but both are used to flavour food. What many don't realise is that spices often contain more disease-fighting antioxidants than some fruits and vegetables but contain no fat, calories, sodium or cholesterol.

Want to know more? Here are some of the best-known healthy spices...

Ginger

For thousands of years this knobbly root has played a role in Chinese, Indian and Middle Eastern medicine, primarily as a digestive aid or to combat all kinds of nausea. More recently ginger has been found to reduce pain and swelling in people with arthritis. Research carried out by the Headache Care Center found that ginger was as effective in reducing migraine pain as conventional medication – 60 per cent of those taking the remedy reported positive results.

Cinnamon

This spice, obtained from the inner bark of cinnamomum trees, is one of the most powerful of the healing spices. It has long been known for its antibacterial and anti-inflammatory properties, but more recently it has been used to improve blood sugar control in people with diabetes. Recent research has discovered that it is high in antioxidants and fibre.

Turmeric

There has been a lot of excitement around the properties of turmeric in recent years. This golden yellow root has long been used in Indian medicine to stimulate the appetite and as a digestive aid, but more recently research on the chemical responsible for turmeric's golden hue (curcumin) has shown it to be an anti-cancer agent.

Nutmeg

Extracted from the kernel of the fruit of the nutmeg tree, the oil found in nutmeg, myristicin, is the same as found in many other plants including carrots, celery and parsley, but in nutmeg it is more concentrated. Like cloves, it also contains eugenol, a compound that may benefit the heart. It has also been found to kill bacteria in the mouth that contribute towards cavities.

Cloves

Dried flower buds from the Myrtaceae tree, this warm and aromatic spice has for centuries been known for its numbing effect and been used to treat toothache. Containing antibacterial properties, clove oil has been found to kill certain bacteria resistant to antibiotics. In one study it was shown to be high in antioxidants, giving potential protection from heart disease, helping fight cancer, and slowing bone and cartilage damage caused by arthritis.

Cardamom

One of history's most expensive spices, cardamom has long been a medicinal staple in the East to treat heart disease, asthma, bronchitis, symptoms of colds and flu, and many digestive problems such as bad breath, colic, constipation and diarrhoea. Containing 25 volatile oils, the most medically active is cineole, which is also found in bay leaves. Recent studies have shown that the oils in cardamom are a powerful anti-inflammatory and antispasmodic, both of which can work together to improve digestion.

Garlic

The potent aroma produced by garlic comes from its most active ingredient, allicin. Because of its versatility it has been studied at length and is believed to help lower blood pressure, keep arteries flexible, lower risk of heart attack, prevent colon and stomach cancer, fight infection and prevent colds. It is also a strong antibacterial, antifungal and can even repel ticks!

Cayenne

Long used as a decongestant, the peppery compound that is found in cayenne (capsaicin) is the active ingredient used in many creams and ointments used to treat arthritis and muscle pain. It is also thought to act as an anti-inflammatory and antioxidant and has been used to treat pain.

As with all complementary medicine we suggest you consult your doctor before taking any of these, especially if you are currently taking conventional medication.

SPICY SMOOTHIES

These healthy smoothies are a delicious way to add more
spice to your diet

Adding a little of your favourite spice can really give a smoothie a boost. Spices
like cinnamon, ginger and cardamom can enhance the main ingredient and
make the smoothie even more delicious! In adding spices, you are adding a
well-rounded, warm or aromatic flavour to your smoothie and some extra
nutrition. Spices have many individual benefits: cinnamon, for example, is
energising and a great healer, ginger is good at preventing colds and flu, while
cardamom is high in antioxidants and minerals.

To make the smoothies
Place all the ingredients into a blender and blend until smooth. To heat the
warm smoothies, transfer to a small pan and gently warm on the hob or put in
a microwavable mug and heat on a medium setting. Make sure it doesn't boil.

Always put the solid ingredients in first and top with liquid if using a blender
where you fill the container and screw on the blade section. For blenders with
the blade in the base, when you put the ingredients into the jug, put the liquid
in first to protect the blades.

Warm spicy chocolate

Slightly chocolatey, quite spicy but not sweet

* ½ avocado
* 1 tbsp cacao or organic cocoa powder
* 1 tsp mixed spice (or favourite spice powder)
* 1 tsp maple syrup or honey
* 350ml skimmed milk

Note: Warm gently to release spice flavour, but do not boil.

Sweet & citrus

Orange and cinnamon with a hint of spinach

* 100g sweet potato (cooked and cold)
* ½ frozen banana
* Handful of spinach
* 1 tsp cinnamon
* 120ml orange juice
* 120ml cold water

Masala banana mix

Thick and creamy mango, with a hint of spice

* 1 frozen banana
* 100g mango (fresh or tinned)
* 1 tsp garam masala
* 1 tsp almond butter
* 150ml coconut milk

Gingerbread warmer

Ginger and banana (lovely warm!)

* 1 banana (not frozen)
* 1 tsp ginger powder
* ½ tsp cinnamon
* 1 tsp almond butter
* 350ml almond milk

Note: Warm gently to release spice flavour, but do not boil.

Orange & cinnamon

Very orangey, thin consistency

* 1 orange (peeled, with pith cut off)
* 2 heaped tbsp vanilla yoghurt
* 1 tsp cinnamon
* Handful of ice cubes
* 120ml orange juice

Spicy nutty potatoes

Mild, creamy and sweet with a hint of spice

* 100g sweet potato (cooked and cold)
* ½ frozen banana
* 1 tsp mixed spice
* 1 tsp almond butter
* 250ml cup almond milk

**Each recipe makes
a single snack serving.**

FANTASY TO FACT

Don't be fooled by the perfect photographs and seemingly happy lives
people lead on social media. Appearances can be deceptive...

When you're at home in your onesie eating chocolate and either doing homework
or binge-watching a Netflix box-set, it's likely that most of your friends are doing
the same. But it only takes one person to post a photo of themselves, out doing
something exciting, to make you feel you should be doing something else.

Similarly, when you look at celebrity photos on Instagram or in magazines, they
look flawless and the stars seem to be leading lavish lives. Even YouTubers, who
are supposed to be 'real', always appear to be doing fun, interesting things. No
wonder it's easy to compare yourself and your life to the photos and stories and
despair that your days aren't jam-packed with fabulous events. But let's face it,
how many people post the regular, everyday stuff – like being half-asleep while
eating breakfast or rummaging through the wardrobe desperately hoping their
favourite shirt is clean? The fact is that mostly what you see isn't reality...

Jealous intentions

If you ever feel jealous of status updates, this will interest you. In a recent survey, 75 per cent of people admitted making their lives sound more exciting on social media. The survey, by phone maker HTC, revealed that more than half of those questioned admitted they posted images of items and places purely to cause jealousy among friends and family. It's no wonder so many can feel depressed going on social media. Scrolling through all those happy status updates, holiday pictures and friends-and-family moments can make people feel down about their own lives, especially when so many teenagers compare themselves to celebrities. But, as with photographs, often you'll only post something big, exciting or a highlight – people don't post about their problems or insecurities.

Digital deception

Filters and phone-editing tools can magically turn an ordinary photograph into something extraordinary. You can remove acne, whiten teeth and make your face look slimmer with the click of a button. #nofilter or #iwokeuplikethis are hashtags often used on a fantastic image, but you never really know what's behind that picture. Trawling through Facebook, Snapchat and Instagram, count how many photos are posed. These are shots that have been thought about – not photos of someone doing the washing up or frantically trying to finish an essay at the last moment. It's rare you'll post a photograph that you don't like, so remember others will think the same.

Different shapes

Do you ever look with envy at how slim many stars are in magazines or on social media? Well, always inspect those images a little more closely as many are photoshopped – or altered – to slim down thighs, waists or faces. When anyone notices an obvious edit, people on social media are quick to point out the weird-shaped arm or butt and embarrass them. Reality star Kim Kardashian faced a huge backlash from fans when paparazzi bikini shots taken of her on a beach seemed to be different to the flawless images she had posted of herself on her sites.

Altered images

Celebrities have a lot of help making them picture perfect. They may have their own stylist, make-up artist, chef, personal trainers and hairdresser and even if they don't, before a photoshoot there will be a team of people helping them look fantastic. Some may even have paid money to improve their appearance. Cosmetic surgery is still a taboo subject, with many celebrities refusing to admit that they've had work done on their face or body, but botox, facelifts and even eyebrow tattoos are easily accessible to stars nowadays.

Faking it for followers

Don't forget that celebrities – as well as non-celebrities – often put posts up to get more followers and likes or views on their channels. Their looks affect their money-making power. Some stars don't even manage their social media – they have a management team to post pictures and status updates to create the perfect image for the public. When they upload posed photographs, that picture isn't necessarily an accurate representation of what's going on. Many celebrities have the same worries as you. They just don't tell everyone about it as they don't want to reveal too much.

Role models

Hollywood actress Kate Winslet got so tired of her images being photoshopped in magazines that she now has no-Photoshop clauses in her contracts. 'It does feel important to me because I do think we have a responsibility to the younger generation of women,' said the star of 1997 movie *Titanic* and a model for international make-up company L'Oreal. 'I think they do look to magazines, I think they do look to women who have been successful in their chosen careers and they want people to look up to. I would always want to be telling the truth about who I am to that generation because they've got to have strong leaders.'

FIVE THINGS TO REMEMBER

* Appearances are rarely what they seem.
* People post their best pictures.
* Few people post the dull, everyday-life stuff.
* Part of a celebrity's mission is to make money.
* A star's talent is more important than what they look like.

10 FOOD AND NUTRITION TRUTHS YOU NEED TO HEAR

Information on food and nutrition is everywhere. From TV to social media to magazines, it can seem impossible to escape people telling you what and when to eat. Even more frustrating is the matter of who to trust when it comes to nutrition advice – there's so much conflicting evidence out there, working out what to believe and act upon can be confusing. Here, a registered dietitian highlights 10 important truths about food and nutrition that are fundamental to everyone enjoying what they eat

1 There's no such thing as healthy and unhealthy foods

Every single food can feature in a healthy balanced diet, and that includes foods traditionally referred to as unhealthy like chocolate, biscuits, cakes and sweets. This is because all foods, irrespective of their nutrient content, contain some sort of goodness – whether it's energy for work and play, simply an amazing taste to nourish your soul at a birthday party or family event or just chilling in front of the TV. It's important not to cut out or be fearful of eating any foods, not only for your health but for a positive relationship with food and a social life, too. For example, when I think of a Friday night in with my girlfriends, the first thing that springs to mind is pizza and ice cream. To make it balanced, I'll add a side salad and the next day I'll serve everyone some fruit with porridge.

2 Sugar isn't bad for you

Although it's a good idea to cut down on sugary, fizzy drinks (which aren't good for teeth health), a bit of sugar is fine. Whatever your preferred sweet food is, enjoy it, without the guilt, in moderation – and this can even be daily in addition to relatively healthy meals. I love sitting down in the evening with my sister and chatting over a cup of strong tea and some chocolate biscuits. Food is much more than just calories – it's about the memories that it helps to create.

3 Not everything you read about nutrition online is true

Although the internet shares many wonderful articles, not all websites are reputable. I recommend NHS Choices (nhs.uk) for nutrition and health information and the British Dietetic Association's food fact sheets (bda.uk.com/foodfacts/home).

4 Not everything you read about food in health magazines is true

Growing up I used to believe everything that I read in magazines about food and diet. It's only in the past 10 years, after qualifying as a dietician, that I now know not all articles can be trusted. Make sure to see who has written the article and/or who is being quoted. Check that they are a dietician or registered nutritionist. The term 'nutritionist' alone isn't a protected title unfortunately, which means that anyone can call themselves a nutritionist, regardless of their (lack of) training, education and experience.

5 You can eat foods that you can't pronounce

It's a myth that you 'shouldn't eat foods that you can't pronounce'. I mean, how many people can say 'quinoa' correctly? Whatever you want to eat for your lunch, whether at school or at home, have the confidence to eat it and don't worry about what others may think. One day you might want a quinoa salad, the next chicken and fries or pasta and garlic bread. Life is about balance and variety.

6 You don't need to eat the same foods or amount as friends or family

There is no such thing as the perfect diet because everyone leads different lives. Try not to be influenced by other people's eating habits and instead eat what you enjoy and what you know will be the right thing for your body.

7 You don't need to calorie count

Calorie counting is unnecessary, time-consuming and zaps almost all of the joy out of eating. People need calories to function and the body is already pretty good at telling you when you need to eat – it's called feeling hungry. Trust your own feelings of fullness and eat when you need to.

8 You shouldn't ever compare your body to other people's

Luckily, nobody looks alike. You are a unique individual and should never compare yourself to others. Everyone comes in different shapes, sizes and heights, which is what makes them so interesting and beautiful. Celebrate yourself for the awesome person that you are – you're so much more than your body.

9 You should celebrate food

People don't just eat food for energy or goodness, they eat because it tastes good, they're socialising, they're with friends or simply because it's being offered. Food should be celebrated for its ability to create an occasion. If you want to learn more about enjoying what food really stands for, try reading *Eat Up!* by Ruby Tandoh.

10 You shouldn't have to sort out your food issues by yourself

If you have any concerns about your food intake, please don't suffer or worry in silence. Speak to your parents, doctor or school counsellor for help and guidance. If you think you may have disordered eating or an eating disorder check out the Beat website at beateatingdisorders.org.uk.

Hopefully you've found this article useful, and remember to enjoy every mouthful of food that you eat today.

EVERYTHING YOU
NEED TO KNOW ABOUT
CAFFEINE

Plenty of people enjoy a coffee-shop stop as part of their daily routine,
happily ordering hot chocolates, colas, cappuccinos and mochas on their
way to college or work – but exactly what's in their drink? It's time to
take a closer look at caffeine...

Are you one of the many thousands who make a daily morning or lunch-time stop at the local café for a quick pick-me-up tea, coffee, cola or even a comfort-giving hot chocolate? If so, the chances are your beverage of choice contains caffeine, a natural physical and mental stimulant. And although small amounts of caffeine are healthy – and if you have it 30 minutes before a workout in particular, it can help to improve physical performance – having too much of it is not a good thing.

There are no official UK recommendations on caffeine consumption for young people, but the European Food Standards Agency advises that daily intakes of up to 3mg of caffeine per kg of body weight do not raise safety concerns. In Canada, it's lower, at 2.5mg of caffeine per 1kg of body weight a day. So, as an example, a 14 year old who weighs 50kg would have an upper daily limit of 150mg of caffeine a day – that's the equivalent of two cups of tea or a cup and a half of instant coffee.

To put 150mg of caffeine into a wider context, here are some other examples of how much caffeine, on average, is in commonly consumed foods and drinks:

* **Coffee-shop coffee** = 100-400mg
* **Instant coffee** = 100mg
* **Black tea** = 75mg
* **100g dark chocolate** = 50mg
* **Can of cola** = 50mg
* **Green tea** = 35mg
* **100g milk chocolate** = 20mg

Consuming too much caffeine can cause sleeping difficulties. It can also bring about increased heart rate, stomach upset, restlessness and mood swings.

If you're worried about whether you might be consuming too much caffeine, the first thing to do is talk to a trusted adult, perhaps a family member, your doctor or the school nurse. Then think about gradually cutting down on caffeine in your diet. Try alternating coffee with a decaf version or choose herbal or fruit teas instead. Don't cut caffeine out all at once, though, as you may experience withdrawal symptoms, which can include headaches.

On a positive note, tea and coffee – decaf or not – count towards your daily fluid intake of eight cups a day, and they provide healthy antioxidants which may help to protect you from future disease (but only when drunk as part of a healthy balanced diet). So don't worry unnecessarily and certainly don't feel you have to remove caffeine totally from your diet. Just be aware of what you're drinking and when – the occasional cup of coffee out with friends is definitely still on the menu.

TIPS ON CUTTING DOWN ON CAFFEINE

Get enough sleep
Younger people are advised to aim for nine to 10 hours of sleep a night. Avoid drinking caffeinated drinks for several hours before going to bed so that it doesn't disrupt your sleep and leave you feeling drowsy the next day. Why? If you're feeling tired, you're more likely to look for a caffeine hit for energy.

Stay hydrated with water
Water should be the go-to drink for hydration as it's both caffeine- and sugar-free (and so much kinder to teeth). Milk also counts towards your fluid intake. The easiest way to tell if you're properly hydrated is to look at the colour of your urine – if it's anything darker than pale straw then you need to drink more.

Look for caffeine-free or lower caffeine containing drinks
As well as green and herbal teas, which contain less caffeine than regular tea, decaffeinated coffee or barley coffee are tasty alternatives.

Have caffeine only when you feel you need it

Whether it's pre-workout or as a pick-me-up, try to keep your intake to no more than 150mg a day (or 3mg per 1kg of body weight). Exercise is great if you're feeling tired as it helps to get your blood and oxygen pumping around your body, so it might be that all you need is a brisk walk rather than another coffee.

Energy drinks are not recommended for younger people and drinks that contain caffeine at a level over 150mg per litre must state 'High caffeine content' on the label. Always look for this warning.

MAKE A CAFFEINE-FREE ICED 'MOCHA'

Makes one cup

* 200ml milk
* Ice cubes
* 1-2 tsp barley coffee or decaf instant coffee
* 20ml off-the-boil water
* 80ml cold water
* 1-2 tsp cocoa powder
* 1-2 tsp sweetener
* ½ tsp cinnamon (optional)

1. Place the milk and a handful of ice cubes into a blender.
2. Dissolve the barley coffee or decaf instant coffee in a dash of hot water. Then top up with cold water to make 100ml. Add the liquid to the blender.
3. Add the cocoa powder, sweetener and cinnamon (if using) to the blender.
4. Whizz it all up.
5. Drink as it is or pour over more ice cubes to make it even cooler.

'I'LL DO IT LATER'

Have you ever put off an important task even though you know deep down it's probably a bad idea? Here's why 'procrastination' can sometimes make you more stressed, not less

There can't be many of you who haven't put homework off for another day, guitar practice for another week or tidying your room for (at least) another month. It's rarely a disaster – there are occasions when there's no option but to delay a task and sometimes it works just as well (if not better) to do it later.

But there's an old saying you might have heard: 'Don't put off until tomorrow what you can do today' and (unfortunately) it does have quite a lot going for it. Why? Because endlessly putting off a task, or 'procrastinating', can increase stress levels and have an effect on your achievements.

Why tomorrow?

Be honest, not all tasks are created equal. Let's say you're given two instructions: 'Tidy your room' and 'Here's some money – order pizzas for you and your friends'. We know which one we'd put to the side. But people procrastinate for many reasons. It could be:

* There's something about a task that is unappealing.
* It compares unfavourably to another activity you could be doing.
* Your feelings around it are negative.

So, you might put off studying for a science test because:
* You don't like the subject.
* You'd rather be with your friends at the park.
* Deep down you're worried that you won't do well.

When is it a problem?

Putting something off until later isn't always an issue (some people even work better when they have a deadline looming). Postponing a task isn't always procrastination, either – like when the dog needs a walk but it's raining heavily so you wait until the weather clears up.

By the same token, short-term procrastination of the 'I just don't feel like it' type may not be a problem – who doesn't hit the snooze button a few times before getting out of bed? When the delay becomes more long term, however, it can have a knock-on effect. This could be when you press snooze too many times, make yourself late and then end up starting your day stressed and frazzled.

Think ahead

Often the problem with procrastination is that it can make tasks seem overwhelming, even the pleasant ones.

Take Christmas presents, for example. Say you have 10 to buy for your friends and you have to hand them all out on the last day of term. You could spend a couple of days thinking about what each friend might like and then buy two each weekend in the five weeks leading up to the festive break. That's two per weekend over five weeks – not so bad.

Delay the task for too long and those numbers creep up. Two becomes four, four turns into six, and then before you know it you have only one weekend to find 10 gifts that you know your friends will like and you're really happy with.

Schoolwork's the same. Suppose you have two weeks to complete an assignment. It's a difficult one and you're not feeling confident about it, so you leave it until later. Before you know it, you have only one week left to do it, which instantly makes it seem even more overwhelming and difficult. Perhaps at this point you put it off further, and end up rushing to get it done the day before the due date. This can result in more stress and possibly a lower mark than the one you could have achieved.

What's the solution?

Realising when procrastination is a problem is the first step to tackling the issue. Take the example of the assignment, for instance. If the stress and (possibly) a lower mark than the one you know you could have achieved dent your confidence, you might repeat the same pattern next time you have a similar test – and, without meaning to, put yourself in an unhelpful cycle or pattern of behaviour.

If, on the other hand, you look at the situation and see that starting the assignment earlier might have meant less stress and a higher mark, then you can decide to change things. The important thing is not to give yourself a hard time. Accept that it happened and try to think of ways to tackle less appealing tasks in the future. Here are a few methods we use at the *Teen Breathe* office...

LET'S GET THIS THING DONE

Manage your time. Create a timetable around activities, whether they're things you want to do (decorate your room) or things you need to do (tidy your desk). It will help to organise yourself in a way that means you fit everything in and manage your time effectively.

Break tasks into blocks. Dividing a large task (studying for that science test next week) into several smaller ones (reading five or six pages a day over a week) makes everything seem more manageable. In a similar way, you could tidy your room area by area over a week or write a paragraph or so of your assignment each day. Start small and things will gain their own momentum.

Rewards. Every time you complete a section of the task, give yourself a break to do something else (sit in the garden with a hot chocolate) but keep an eye on timings.

If you still leave something until the last minute, remember – 'better late than never'. See it as a challenge and do your best (read your whole science book in two days and hope you remember some of it).

10 FREE WAYS TO EXERCISE IN 10 MINUTES OR LESS

Regular exercise doesn't have to be expensive. If you can't afford a gym membership, here are 10 ways to get moving that won't break the bank...

1 Early morning moving!
The thought of getting up earlier than usual for school might sound unappealing, but it will be worth it. Set your alarm 10 minutes early, go for a quick walk, run or put some music on and get dancing. It will lift your mood for the rest of the day as well as boosting energy levels.

2 Salute the sun
Yoga isn't just about bending and stretching your body into strange shapes. It's a great way to exercise and helps people manage stress. You can start with what is called the Sun Salutation, which only takes a few minutes. It's a great way to stretch out after a night's sleep and greet the day.

3 Walk whenever possible

If it's safe to do so, why not walk or cycle to school instead of getting a lift in the car or catching a bus? You might be surprised at what you see on the way.

4 Fitness with friends

Instead of texting your friends, snapchatting or playing video games with them, meet up and play a quick game of your favourite sport outside. Fitness is much more fun with friends... and even if they don't want to go for a walk or run, your dog will love you for taking them out (don't have a pooch in the family? You could offer to walk a neighbour's dog).

5 Tidy time

Helping parents with the chores may be boring, but think of the fitness benefits. Consider how far you walk while vacuuming or how much effort you put into cleaning the car. The more effort you put in, the better for your fitness. Next time you're cleaning upstairs, don't collect all the things to take up in one go – run up and down every time you need an item. It won't take that much extra time but it will burn calories, work your legs and think of the extra brownie points you'll get from your parents.

6 Make a hot drink

Why waste the time it takes for the water to boil when making your coffee or tea? Pick up a couple of soup cans and do some bicep curls, run on the spot, do some squats or try the plank exercise. See if you can keep it up until the steam whistle blows (or the electric kettle switches off).

7 Lunch break

Lunch breaks mean precious time with your friends – but why not suggest you all join one of the school clubs or, if there aren't any you like, find out how you could start one you would enjoy? If you and your friends are competitive, why not start a fitness challenge with other students? A little healthy competition always spurs people on.

8 Box fit

Addicted to TV box-sets? If you really can't tear yourself away from Netflix, consider exercising in front of the TV. You could do sit-ups, the plank, floor exercises or stretches and turn that TV time into toning time.

9 Go outdoors

Spend 10 minutes towards the end of the day helping your parents watering plants, weeding or doing any little chores that need to be done. It will gently get you moving and impress your family at the same time.

10 Bedtime yoga

Downward-facing Dog, Triangle Pose and Seated Spinal Twist are just some of the yoga poses that can help you relax and sleep more soundly – look up evening yoga exercises online for more poses and instructions. Follow up your practice with a meditation or awareness session and you're bound to enjoy sweet dreams and wake up bright, fit and ready for anything next morning.

IT'S GOOD TO TALK

It may not always be easy talking to a parent or guardian – they might come across as overly critical, while you feel awkward even beginning a conversation – but it can be worth it...

Occasionally it can feel like you're on the exact same wavelength as a parent or guardian and other times it can feel like they don't understand the first thing about you. Even though there's plenty of times you need them and their help or advice, sometimes when you try to speak to them it just comes out as anger and frustration. The good news is that there are plenty of things you can do about this to help one of those talks run more smoothly.

When you want something

Starting a conversation with 'I really want...' or 'Everyone else has...' is unlikely to get a parent onside. Let them know this isn't an on-the-spot decision about something you need: this is an issue you've been thinking about for some time. Give thought-through, logical reasons why you need this thing – for example, you'd like to feel good about yourself by wearing something new; you'd like some games that would help you relax when you're not studying; or you'd really like to go to the festival because you feel it would help increase your independence. Importantly, explain how you could contribute to or repay any cash. If you've worked out that from your Saturday job you can give £25 or you're going to spend the next two months saving towards it, that shows you've given it thought. It'll be harder for them to argue against a sensible, logical plan.

When you need help with your emotions

Maybe you haven't received the exam results you'd hoped for or you've argued with a friend. It might not always feel like it, but parents and guardians want nothing more than to be included and help when big stuff happens. At times like this it may be hard to plan a calm conversation – perhaps tears and emotions might take over, but this is okay. Just tell them what happened and what's upset you. Giving them clues on how they can support you (or not) can be useful, too: 'I'm not sure what I want to do about this just yet,' or 'It would be really nice if we could just watch a film together tonight and forget about all of this for a while.'

When you feel like you're not being told something

Sometimes you just know information is being kept from you – and you're sure it's important. The chances are they feel it's either too big or inappropriate to tell you, or they don't know how to deal with it themselves. A 'grown-up' approach is key here but it's got to be genuine. Let them know that you've noticed they're distracted or untalkative and ask if they're okay. They might be looking for the right time to tell you something. And if you can't do anything else, maybe leave a little note or gift for them – to let them know you're thinking of them.

When you're in trouble

Whether you've broken a valuable ornament or have a detention at school, you know you've got to come clean. Sit with a parent or guardian and let them know there's something you need to tell them. Open with the fact that you may be disappointed in yourself, but don't sugar-coat what's happened – give it to them straight. Give an indication that you know how they might be feeling hearing this: 'I know this will be a shock or disappointment.' Then tell them your plan for sorting out the situation – how you can fix or replace an item, for example, or how you've spoken to your teacher about completing extra schoolwork.

And if all else fails...

If you've tried all the tips above and you're still not getting anywhere, don't think that you've failed. It might be that a parent or guardian has just too much going on and can't make themselves available to you right now. Try again another time when you think that they might be in a better mood to listen. If this doesn't get you any further, you still don't have to give up. You could consider finding another adult you trust enough, perhaps an auntie or uncle, to talk to in the meantime.

SOME GENERAL GUIDANCE

* Try to talk about important things when you're feeling calm and have time – not as you're rushing off somewhere.
* It can feel more comfortable to talk when you're side by side, such as when you're in the car or walking.
* Remember your parent/guardian is human too – there will be times when they feel tired, stressed or worried, so these are times to maybe avoid a 'big' talk.
* Blaming doesn't help anyone – try to take responsibility for what's happened and how you're feeling. Instead of starting statements with 'You...' try leading with 'I...' statements, such as 'I feel...'

DAYDREAM BELIEVER

Does your mind have a tendency to wander or zone out? Having your 'head in the clouds' isn't always a bad thing. In fact, when you use the time consciously, daydreaming can be of great benefit

Daydreaming is a bit like taking a mini-holiday from reality – even if just for a few moments. Your imagination can take you anywhere, and you might see your future self as highly successful or even famous. By zoning out, you can imagine all kinds of wonderful possibilities for yourself – and this can feel exciting, uplifting and exhilarating. It's thought that people who regularly set aside time to daydream can benefit emotionally, intellectually and creatively. Daydreaming is a kind of default mode for the mind and it often happens when you're relaxed. But you might also drift off into a dream-world when what you're doing is laborious, repetitive, boring, too challenging, too easy or simply doesn't hold your interest for long

enough. Have you ever found yourself mentally drifting away to a fantasy-land full of wonder and exciting sights while doing the washing up or watching a dull TV show? When you're on autopilot, perhaps when you're making your bed or brushing your teeth, daydreaming is perfectly fine. It can become a problem, however, if your mind starts drifting when you really need to pay attention – during an exam, interview or the sharing of important information.

Living in a dream-world?

When you daydream too much – gazing out the window as minutes slip by – or your mind wanders so that you forget what you've just read or can't recall what someone has said to you, this can have a negative effect. Too much daydreaming means you're most likely not focusing on the task in hand. If you find you daydream at less-than-ideal times – in lessons or even during conversations – try to work out why. For example, if your mind wanders while reading a book, perhaps it's because the subject doesn't engage you or the text is too easy or too difficult. Being aware of when and why you daydream will help you highlight issues, so you can take action to ensure you're fully present when it matters.

GREAT WAYS TO DAYDREAM

Set aside 10 to 20 minutes a day
Identify the perfect time when you'll be on your own without any distractions. This could be while on a bus journey, walking or waiting in a queue, or it might be when you're sitting on a park bench or spending some time at the beach. The best space might be in the comfort of your own room with a zesty tea or hot chocolate (marshmallows optional).

Relax
Get cosy. Sink into the peace and stillness. Breathe calmly and consciously, and let the chatter of everyday thoughts drift away. Soften your gaze or close your eyes, if that feels right.

Think about what you want from your daydream
Maybe you need space to consider your life, relationships, aspirations and goals and to visualise what you would like to achieve. Perhaps you want to work through your feelings, ideas and possibilities or find starting points for a story, piece of art or a creative project. Try to focus on positive daydreaming that nurtures, uplifts and inspires you.

Think of something that will fire your creativity
Daydreams can be sparked by what you see around you, or perhaps there's a picture, poem, story, film or piece of music that really captures your imagination. Let these prompts take you into dreamland.

When you're ready, return to the present moment
Where did your daydreaming take you? How will it inspire and motivate you? What positive ideas or wisdom can you glean? Make some sketches and notes in your journal. You can look back on this later. You might find that your daydreams are just pure fantasy and escapism, but there may well be a gem or two that you can carry forward into your life. Remember, dreams can and sometimes do come true.

'IT ALL STARTS WITH A DREAM'

Anonymous

WHY DAYDREAMING IS GOOD FOR YOU

It boosts your imagination and creativity. You can dream up interesting ideas, inventions and solutions that you can use in creative projects.

It exercises and improves the brain. Daydreaming gives your brain an effective workout and is thought to boost cognitive function.

It encourages emotional wellbeing. By imagining yourself or others in alternative scenarios, it can give you a better appreciation and outlook on a situation and help you resolve your feelings.

It aids achievement of goals and ambitions. You can use your dream-time to inspire and motivate you by imagining a desired outcome and focusing on steps you can take to realise your long-held ambitions.

EMOTIONAL AWARENESS

Just like thoughts, emotions come and go throughout the day. But a lot of the time, it's all too easy not to be aware of them or to really know and understand *what* you're feeling

Can you think of a time when you just felt 'off' – when something was bothering you or didn't feel right, but you weren't really sure what it was? You might have had a niggling sense of disquiet as you ate breakfast, went to classes and milled around at lunchtime. And then, towards the end of the day, a little event that shouldn't have been a big deal made you really angry and you overreacted.

Be reassured that everyone has had such a day. Often, the reason for the sense of unease is not really knowing what you're feeling… and if you can't notice and deal with emotions, they stick with you for a long time and can make you upset. They can even make you behave in ways that are out of proportion or inappropriate. The good news is there are ways to tap into your feelings and learn how to manage them.

How can you be more aware of your emotions and work through them? Try some of these suggestions and see if they help...

Listen to your body

Although you usually view emotions as being in your head, almost all of them can be felt somewhere in your body. Just think about the expression 'having a heavy heart' for when someone is sad or 'butterflies in the stomach' for when a person is nervous.

Practise tuning in to your body to see if you can work out where you feel different emotions. For example, you can see if you notice sensations like tightness, heaviness, lightness, tingling or movement. Do you clench your jaw, sigh or fidget a lot when you have certain feelings?

This can be tricky at first because you may not be used to thinking about emotions in this way. But you might start to realise, for example, that when your shoulders become tight or hunched, it's a sign that you're worried. That means you've become more aware of your emotions.

Name your emotion

Neuroscientists, whose area of study includes the brain and emotions, say that when you can label a feeling – be it happy, sad or angry – it loses some of its charge and you don't feel so overwhelmed by it.

The next time you notice you're reacting to something, try to name your emotion. Don't worry about getting the perfect word for what you're feeling – just see if you can label what's happening.

See your emotions as information

It's easy to think of emotions as being positive or negative, but it can be helpful to see them simply as information – whether they be good, bad or indifferent. An emotion is just your body's way of telling you that something around you needs your attention. For example, when you hear a sudden loud noise, you feel scared. You become more alert so you can investigate what's happening and take action if necessary.

It can be fascinating to think about emotions this way. Instead of getting wrapped up in what you are feeling, ask yourself: 'What information is my body sending me? What needs my attention right now?'

Observe your emotion

Did you know that emotions only last about 90 seconds? Just like thoughts, they will eventually fade and go away.

If you can, try watching the emotion – noticing what it feels like, what thoughts pop up in your mind, if there are any impulses to do something, how fast or slow the emotion is and how it fades away.

When you start to become more aware of your feelings, you create space for yourself to process them. You can then respond to situations in better ways (instead of overreacting or doing something you might regret later). It's an important skill that helps in all walks of life.

BODY LANGUAGE

Think about the emotions below and how they make themselves known in your body – the sensations they create, their effect on your posture, if they make you frown – and consider how you might react to them.

happy / worried / restless / disappointed / excited / sad / jealous / peaceful / scared

MINDFUL BODY SCAN

Create a close relationship with your body with this simple exercise

1. Slowly let your eyes close, listen to your breathing and feel where your body makes contact with the floor or the bed. Every time you breathe out, feel your body sink a little deeper into the floor.
2. Starting with your head, feel its weight as it rests on the cushion. Now include your forehead, letting it relax. Notice your eyes, nose, cheeks, mouth, chin and ears. If your mind wanders, gently guide it back to the part of the body you are focusing on.
3. Slowly release the focus on your head and face and move your awareness to your neck and shoulders. Notice the strong muscles in this part of the body. If you feel any worry or tension, breathe in and let it go as you breathe out, releasing the sensation from your body.
4. Now move your awareness to your shoulders and the places where they touch the floor or the bed. Extend your focus into your arms, elbows, wrists, hands and fingers and concentrate on your breath.
5. Turn your attention to your chest, noticing the subtle rise and fall with each in and out breath you take. Feel the ribcage, the sides of the ribs and your upper back resting on the floor or bed.

6. Put your hands on your belly and really feel each breath. Focus on your lower back, feeling the gentle pressure as it touches the floor before moving on to your pelvis, hip bones and sitting bones. Be aware of your breath, slowly breathing in and out.
7. Bring your focus gently down to your legs. Feel their weight from the tops of your thighs, right down to your ankles, gently notice the way they rest on the floor.
8. Finally, move your attention to your feet, the soles, the heels and then each of your toes – the big toe, the little toe and the ones in between. Breathe in and gently feel your breath as it moves down your body and into your toes, then breathe out, feeling it coming back up again.
9. Take one or two deeper breaths in and out, filling your whole body, then spend a few minutes lying on the floor. Relax and be aware of your body as a whole, breathing freely.

This exercise should take about 15 minutes, so make yourself comfortable in a room where you won't be disturbed. Lie on your back on the floor or on your bed. You might want to cover yourself with a blanket so you don't get too cold and rest your head on a cushion or pillow for comfort.

TAP THE 'UNFOLLOW' BUTTON

When is it time for you to stop following people on social media?

How many hours a day do you spend looking at other people's posts? You can follow anyone online nowadays – family, friends, celebrities, bloggers, vloggers and sites for things you're interested in, whether it's meditation, teacup dogs or one of the Kardashians. But what happens when you start cringing at some of the things people you follow write, or feel uncomfortable about the posts appearing in your timeline? When is it really time to 'unfollow' people?

FIVE SIGNS YOU NEED TO UNFOLLOW

1 You're annoyed by their posts

If you find yourself getting irritated by certain posters, for whatever reason, it could be time to unfollow. For example, if you're annoyed by the constant selfies, their comments, their hashtags... that annoyance is a waste of your energy. Let them continue their life happily posting what they're posting and doing what they're doing but don't waste your life being irritated.

2 You start comparing your life to theirs

When people post constantly about their seemingly amazing social lives and new purchases and you start feeling jealous, consider switching off. If it's a jealousy you can laugh off, that's fine, but if it makes you feel bad about your own life, it's definitely time to unfollow. It's also worth remembering that most people's lives aren't actually as great as they make out on social media, but if you're comparing your world to theirs, delete.

3 You're made to feel uncomfortable

You may want to hit the unfollow button if someone you follow starts posting inappropriate comments, photos or jokes that leave you feeling uncomfortable. It could be that you don't agree with their viewpoint or the way they are treating someone or singling them out. Would you be friends with that kind of person in real life? Will you miss them if you don't follow them?

4 You're addicted to their drama

If you waste many hours of your day checking on their stories, refreshing your timeline to see if they've posted and using up lots of brainspace thinking about what's going on in their lives, delete them. If they're getting in the way of your actual friendships, consider the time you are spending on people you don't really know or won't ever meet. You'll be surprised how much better you'll feel once you've deleted their dramas from your timeline.

5 You're tempted to make negative comments

If you're so annoyed by someone you're tempted to write a negative comment on their story, it could be time to click that unfollow button. It's fine to disagree with someone's views or even dislike them because of what they're posting, but there's no need to be unpleasant. Delete them and let them get on with it. Turning your back on them and their lives will allow you to get on with yours. You wouldn't go up to a stranger in the street and be nasty, so try not to become a keyboard warrior.

HOW TO UNFOLLOW

Look at the list of people or sites you follow and consider which of them are affecting you the most. Wait a day or two. Then, if they're still having a negative impact, it's time to remove them. One reason not to be too hasty is that you may unfollow someone and then want to follow them again and, if it's someone you know, it could be awkward explaining why you took them off in the first place.

If you feel nervous about removing people, start by deleting a few at a time – you'll be surprised at how much better you feel. Remember, most of the time they won't even notice you're gone.

When it's people you follow who have thousands of followers already, it's as simple as clicking the unfollow button – they're unlikely to know or care.

If it's someone you know on Instagram, they won't be notified you've unfollowed them. If, however, they ever check their followers – and actually pay enough attention – then they may notice. If this happens, consider how you might discuss it with them if they bring it up. Are they a 'real' friend who you'd miss from your life? Or are you just following them out of habit?

Benefits of unfollowing

Your 'feed' on social media is your space. Keep in mind that you're in control of the people you interact with and what you read and post. You can follow anyone you want. Once you've decided what should be in your feed, take time to remember the benefits of social media and ensure you're following the people and sites that inspire you rather than the ones that leave you with negative emotions.

AGE-GAP BUDDIES

You may come from a family where your grandparents always seem to be around, helping out in some way whenever they can. Alternatively, perhaps they live so far away that they can only visit infrequently. As with most things in life, it's the quality, not the quantity that's important. Having a close relationship with grandparents when you do see them is what really matters – and some research suggests this bond can positively influence how you feel overall.

How can these particular relationships have a positive influence on your wellbeing?

* Relationships with grandparents are often very different to the ones you have with your parents. You might feel more able to open up to them about some of the things that are bothering you and they might have more time to listen to you and give you attention when you need it most.

* When things aren't going so well at home, grandparents can also act as a buffer against the circumstances, helping you to catch your breath for a moment and cope. Close relationships between younger and older generations can also help both groups to better understand the issues and challenges that each is facing. It's mutually beneficial.

* You can learn a lot about navigating the ups and downs of life from people who have already been there and done it. They can share with you how they got through it all.

* Being connected to older generations within your family can also give you a greater understanding of what makes you the way you are (did you get your nose or wicked sense of humour from Granny or Grandpa?) and a broader picture of your family background. For example, you may find out more about what your parents were like growing up, the trials and tribulations they went through, helping you to appreciate them better during trickier times.

What's in it for older people?

Life for some people, especially those who are older, can be lonely. If they have few social interactions it can affect their wellbeing. Many take pride and joy in spending time with their grandchildren, and often love hearing about what they've been up to recently. Research suggests that intergenerational contact and shared activities boosts the emotional and mental wellbeing of older people.

What if your grandparents are no longer around or contact with them isn't possible?

Perhaps your grandparents aren't alive any more, or there are historical family reasons why you might not be able to strengthen your relationship with them. This is when building bonds with people from an older generation – even when there are no family ties – can bring benefits of its own.

Care homes for older people often offer volunteering opportunities. These are not only great experiences to add to your CV, but you'll also feel good, knowing that you are contributing positively to someone else's day. Older neighbours are another area for offering potential support and developing friendships and those with little or no local family may appreciate and benefit from help with shopping or assistance in caring for their pets.

Emotional takeaway

Taking time out of your day to spend with older relatives or members of your community is a win-win situation. The benefits both for their wellbeing and yours are clear. The long-lasting sense of pride and satisfaction from giving time to someone else can also help build your own sense of self-esteem and give you an important insight that you can then carry with you into your own older years.

Tips for strengthening your relationship with your grandparents:

* You could ask your grandparents over for lunch (if it's not too far or inconvenient for them to travel to you) or arrange a date to visit them and spend some uninterrupted time chatting. If you have a shared interest, such as supporting the same football team or having a mutual TV show you love to watch, this is a great starting point and a natural springboard to enjoying your time together.

* Being interested in the lives they lived when they were your age is also a good way to get to know them better. You may even be able to arrange a nostalgic day out with them. If your grandparent is technologically savvy, regular texts, emails or social media contact can let them know that you're thinking about them (and, of course, you can share your technological skills with them too). Otherwise, try traditional letter writing. It's a tried and tested way to brighten up anybody's day and show you care.

Don't forget that your parents can often be the 'gatekeepers' to your contact with your grandparents, so it may be a good idea to let them know first that you would like to see your grandparents more. It could be a way to bring the whole family closer together.

A LIGHT TOUCH

Caring for loved ones is admirable and part and parcel of life, but sometimes it's possible to stray into overprotective territory

Imagine you welcome a young puppy into your home. You'll want to care for your precious pet the best you can. You'll look after her by making sure she has enough food and water, play with her, stroke her and take her for walks, plus house-train your pup and remove any potential dangers from your home and garden. Feeling so safe and supported in this caring environment, a puppy will thrive.

But what happens if you take this caring a little too far? Perhaps you're so worried the puppy will run away, you never let her off the leash. So, she never learns good recall or how to play with other dogs safely. You might never let her near water as you're so anxious she'll have an accident. So, if she does ever fall into a pond she won't be able to cope as she's never had the chance to feel comfortable in water. By protecting your puppy too much, she won't be able to develop necessary life skills.

People can behave in similar ways towards their close friends, siblings or other family members. Caring for others usually comes from a good place – you want to shield your loved ones from negative experiences and emotions such as hurt, embarrassment or unhappiness. However, if caring ends up tipping over into overprotectiveness, it no longer benefits you or the person you so dearly care about. Say a friend excitedly announces she's going to audition for a drama production. You're concerned she'll totally embarrass herself and won't cope if she's rejected, so you talk her out of her plans. Or imagine your brother wants to try out abseiling. You're worried he'll seriously injure himself, so you convince him not to go. In reality, people need to make mistakes and learn from their experiences, whether positive or negative.

Avoiding anything challenging limits opportunities to grow in self-confidence. Never experiencing disappointment, difficulty or rejection means fewer chances to develop the resilience needed to cope with life's many ups and downs. If somebody around you feels you're being overprotective or stopping them from living their life, they might start to resent this. In their eyes, it might look like you're trying to control or dominate them. It can also affect the overprotector, making them anxious and fretful. If this sounds like you, try to identify where your feelings come from. For example, are you afraid you'll lose a close friend to a new hobby or different friendship group? It takes self-awareness to recognise the root cause, but it can lead to more positive solutions for everybody. Of course, there are times when you genuinely feel somebody you care about is putting themselves at risk. You wouldn't, for example, let your new puppy loose near a fast-flowing river just to give her a new experience. If you think a friend is going to do something that has the potential to harm themselves or others, it's important to seek guidance from a trusted source.

How do you offer supportive, rather than overprotective, care? If your puppy ran back to you after being bitten by a larger dog in the local park, you wouldn't say: 'I told you so', would you? You'd rush her to the vet for medical help and then concentrate on building up her confidence when around other dogs in the future. People need similar support. If an experience proves particularly challenging, be there to support your friend. Help them to make sense of what happened, identify the positives in the situation and gain the confidence to try again. Friends who care, support and encourage others to follow their own path are valuable indeed.

Caring might be overprotectiveness if you:

* Step in to stop others trying new experiences.
* Dissuade others from doing what they want.
* Focus only on the negatives ('You might fail', 'Other people might laugh').
* Attempt to shield others from potentially unpleasant or difficult experiences.
* Try to fix problems rather than letting others figure out their own solutions.
* Limit others' independence.
* Worry incessantly.

WHAT TO DO IF...

...you feel you're becoming overprotective:

1. **Be kind to yourself**. It's good to care about others, and the ability to recognise any overprotective tendencies is a real positive.
2. **Understand yourself**. Are you afraid you'll lose a friend or miss out? If so, what can you do? Perhaps it's time to try a new hobby? Can you view the situation differently? An expanded friendship group can bring all sorts of benefits.
3. **Get support**. If worrying about others is stopping you sleeping and relaxing, or if you think somebody is in danger, speak to a trusted adult or contact a service such as Childline (childline.org.uk).

...you feel a friend or sibling is overprotective towards you:

1. **Be kind**. Remember: caring comes from good intentions.
2. **Listen**. There might be valid concerns you need to consider.
3. **Include them**. Worries might come from a fear of being left out or pushed aside. See if your friend would like to join you or encourage them in their own pursuits.
4. **Be assertive**. Thank them for their concern and explain calmly why you think the experience will be good for you.

Is your overprotectiveness holding back those you care for most?
Try to let them learn from their mistakes.

THE GREAT OUTDOORS

Don't fall into the trap of staying indoors when the weather turns cooler –
getting out into the fresh air is just as magical during autumn and winter

Being outside feels so effortless in the summer, doesn't it? As well as warm sun
and blue skies, there's lots going on and longer days in which to enjoy it all – not
to mention the weeks and weeks away from school and homework. It can be a
carefree time of year. So, it may come as something of a shock to the system when
the afternoons begin to get chillier and darker. During the autumn and winter
term, it often seems like the day is almost over the moment school is out and it
will soon be the season when you might want nothing more than to head straight
home to get warm and cosy. Darker evenings can also have an effect on your
energy levels, causing you to feel drowsy and sluggish. Suddenly, that comfy sofa
has never looked so good. Precisely because of these things, it's important to get
outside all year round. Yes, a little more effort and a few more layers of clothes may
be required, but it'll be well worth it.

Why not just stay in?

Time outdoors, in any season, has been shown to have significant benefits for health and wellbeing, improving memory and reducing feelings of stress and anxiety – all of which is useful when you have homework or assignments to do. The benefits can be long-lasting, too. Believe it or not, research has even shown that young people who spend time outside have better eyesight than those who don't. Colder temperatures tend to signal the beginning of 'sniffle season' – suddenly, everyone seems to have a runny nose or a cough. But did you know that being in fresh air reduces the likelihood of catching a bug? Germs breed and multiply in warm, enclosed areas, so getting out and about can blow all the nasties away. In addition, research has shown that being outside in nature boosts your immune system, helping you to swerve those colds and flus.

Spending time in natural light is vital, because it aids your sleep cycles, meaning that you wake up feeling more refreshed. It also plays a role in maintaining vitamin D levels, which are essential for strong bones, teeth and muscles – so when there are fewer hours of daylight available, try to make the most of them, especially at weekends. Being outdoors means you're more likely to be physically active, which is great news for your fitness levels and overall wellbeing. And, if you needed any more convincing to get out and about, the autumn months are some of the most visually spectacular to be outdoors – the golden light and changing leaves can be truly magical to witness.

LET'S GO OUTSIDE

Get dressed
'There's no such thing as bad weather, just poor clothing choices' – that's how the saying goes and it's absolutely true. Yes, summer wardrobes are fun and colourful, but it's easy to fall in love with chunky, cosy sweaters, warm boots and hats, mittens and scarves – you might even try knitting your own.

Get moving
The chillier months provide an ideal opportunity to stay warm through physical activity. Going for a walk gives you the chance to spend quality time with family and friends outside. The parks are often less crowded too, so make the most of having the swings to yourself.

Get gathering
Collecting glossy, shiny conkers never stops being satisfying, no matter how old you are. Or you could opt for gathering late-season fruits. Don't forget to take a container with you so that you can carry your finds home. Plus, of course, you might want to get your hands on a pumpkin for Halloween.

Get inspired

Nature is at its colourful best right now, so let it spark your creativity and ignite your imagination:

* Have you ever tried making a leaf picture? Gathering fallen leaves and arranging them into an artwork on the ground is fantastic fun, especially as you race to get it completed before a gust of wind disrupts your efforts. A lion is a good one to begin with – those autumn leaves are wonderfully mane-worthy.
* Take your camera out with you and start snapping – experiment with different perspectives and close-ups of natural objects or try some landscape shots of the season in all its glory. The sun is lower in the sky at this time of year, too, so there's more chance of getting a dramatic and beautiful flare in your photo.
* Pack a flask, paper and pencils. Find a comfortable spot from which to take in your surroundings and try to capture your impressions of them, whether in words or hand-drawn images. Don't forget to wrap yourself in an extra layer or two so you don't get cold.

Get cosy

Marshmallows? Check. Drinking chocolate and milk? Check. A warm change of clothes, a favourite blanket, thick socks? Check, check and check. You'll enjoy your time outside even more if you know that you have an inviting and comfortable space to come back to, so make preparations before you leave the house.

IT'S OKAY TO PLAY

Throw aside any notions that playtime is too childish – it's an opportunity to let your hair down, bond with others and lift everyone's spirits

Think back to the time when you were a five-year-old, what was your favourite toy? And what's your favourite toy now? It might seem a strange question to ask as most people think of toys as being something only very young children play with, but if you replace the word 'toy' with 'hobby' or 'game' it might have a different feel.

Sometimes, as people grow up, they develop the idea that playing is just for children, but actually, pretty much everyone has an interest they find fun, whether it's making things, solving puzzles or participating in a sport.

What's meant by 'play'?

It's easy to scoff at the word, but play is just having fun doing things you enjoy. It doesn't matter what they are. The key words here are fun and enjoy because play is about doing something for pleasure. Growing up and becoming more sophisticated doesn't rule that out. If you think about it, so-called grown-ups play all the time, whether it's video games, sports, flying drones, drawing or canoeing.

Why play's important

Life can be hectic, and it's easy to forget to factor in light-hearted moments. Too often, people stop doing things they used to enjoy as they become overwhelmed by other commitments or get hooked on social media, but play is a crucial part of life. Young children develop social skills while playing, and it's often the ultimate treat. The same applies to adults when they socialise or let their hair down (have you ever noticed how much grown-ups love playing on the swings in a playground?).

Make it spontaneous...
Whether it's a spur-of the moment game of football, a jamming session in the music room or video-editing and coding in the IT department, spend time with friends doing something you enjoy. It's not about winning, or needing to finish a task, it's about relaxing and enjoying an activity for no reason other than joy.

...or have a plan
Arrange something you know will be low-key, enjoyable and give your friends a boost – it could be playing cards, singing, even a game of I Spy. But again, no expectations and no need to accomplish a task.

Ignore anyone who mocks
At some point, there'll be people who try to mock your hobby or game – ignore them. There's no rule that says you have to stop doing what you love at a certain age – whether it's putting on drama productions, making model aeroplanes or playing a sport.

Don't let others persuade you that 'it's for kids' and 'you should grow out of it'. This isn't true. Be different. Continue to play and spend time on toys, hobbies, pastimes – call them what you will – that give you pleasure. Even better, surround yourself with other equally smart folk who also know that it's okay to have fun.

KEEP IT LIGHT

Take a phone break

It's common for people to lose hours while scrolling on their mobile phones. But too much time spent on social media can have a negative impact on how you feel about yourself. If you have a phone, take breaks and allow yourself some time to play in another way. Of course, there are many ways you can use your phone to enjoy games, apps or puzzles, but take a digital detox every once in a while and enjoy outdoor pastimes with other people.

Don't rush to be older

You've probably heard your parents or guardians say 'don't wish your life away' and thought 'how dull is that', especially when you want to be old enough to have more independence and freedom to do what you want.

Truth is, they might be onto something (sorry!). Homework and school projects aside, most students have few commitments, but a time will come when this will change. The reason adults say to enjoy playing and being young is because they know this moment will arrive all too quickly (even though right now it might seem like it's ages away).

Play with others

Younger kids may be annoying at times, but they'll love you playing games with them (remember when you were younger and had a babysitter or someone you looked up to who played games with you?) and chances are you'll have fun, even if you do find their games childish.

Don't forget that older relatives might also enjoy sharing a game or puzzle. And your pets, especially dogs, will always want to play. Playing is an easy way to make others happy and boost your own self-confidence by doing something positive for another person.

'THE TIME TO RELAX IS WHEN YOU DON'T HAVE TIME FOR IT'

Sydney J Harris

NATURAL FILTERS

Plants can do so much more for your home than make it look pretty – many will make the air you breathe cleaner and some can even add some much-needed moisture...

Not satisfied with simply adding splashes of colour and lifting a room out of the gloom, houseplants naturally filter out toxins and microbes that lurk in your home. The chemicals associated with paint, dry cleaning and carpet manufacturing are absorbed into their leaves, while mould spores and bacteria are suppressed by the release of phytochemicals. They also humidify the dry air in our centrally heated houses. Some are better than others at doing this job, so here's a list of the ones that work hardest to make your rooms more breathable…

Ivy

According to Nasa, the evergreen ivy tops the list as best air-filtering houseplant. It is robust, easy to care for and acclimatises to most conditions. It is best grown in moderate conditions, out of direct sunlight.

Peace Lily

This is the most effective plant at removing the common household chemicals found in paint and carpets. It is also very easy to care for and lets you know when it needs watering by drooping its leaves slightly.

Rubber Plant

An evergreen that originates from India, the rubber plant is a good all-rounder with excellent toxin-eliminating qualities. It thrives well in cooler, shady corners, but may require some pruning to stop it from getting too big.

Bamboo Palm

A beautiful plant that adds elegance to any room, the bamboo palm has the extra benefit of keeping a room humidified. It can grow up to 1.8m, so choose its position well and make sure it is where air circulates freely to deter spider mites.

Dracaena

This group of plants is wide and varied, offering a solution to pretty much any condition. The red-edged dracaena can grow up to 4.5m and is best in sunlight. All dracaenas need moist soil and benefit from a monthly feed with an all-purpose liquid fertiliser.

Aloe Vera

Known as 'The Plant of Immortality' by the Egyptians, this easy-to-grow succulent is happy to sit on a sunny windowsill. If brown spots appear it is letting you know toxin levels are getting too high. The gel inside has the added benefit of helping to heal cuts and burns.

Golden Pothos

Virtually indestructible, this plant is great if you are prone to forgetting to water them! It is considered one of the best all-round air purifiers with its ability to absorb many toxins. It has a trailing habit, so works well in indoor hanging baskets. The only thing it won't tolerate is direct sunlight.

Weeping Fig

A beautiful plant that makes a statement in a room but it can be temperamental. It is great at filtering out pollutants that typically accompany carpet and furniture manufacturing, but the conditions have to be just right. It is best grown in bright, but indirect light and it doesn't like temperature fluctuations.

WRITE TO EXPRESSION

More often than not it's great to be honest and speak your mind – but there are certain times when it's best to keep your thoughts to yourself. This doesn't mean you can't express what you're really thinking and feeling – just pick up a pen and get writing or drawing

Have you ever wanted to say something that you know you really shouldn't? Have you ever experienced thoughts or feelings that you felt embarrassed about or ashamed of? It might have been shouting 'I hate you' at a sibling or telling a parent that you 'didn't ask to be born'. It might have felt liberating to express yourself in that exact moment, but later you might have felt bad about what you said because you know you didn't really mean it and it isn't true.

When people get angry or upset, the prefrontal cortex – the part of the brain responsible for rational thinking and processing language – doesn't work as well. The energy in the brain becomes concentrated in its emotional centre and this puts you fully in feeling mode. This is why you might end up thinking or saying things you don't really mean, because the language part of the brain isn't working well enough for you to be able to properly filter your words. Although it's not always helpful to say hurtful things in the heat of the moment, it's good to acknowledge your feelings. There's nothing wrong with you for feeling angry, hurt, sad, jealous or frustrated. Negative thoughts and feelings aren't something to be ashamed of, they naturally occur without your conscious control.

Processing your emotions

You do, however, have control over the way you process your feelings. If you spend time biting your tongue and being unable to express your thoughts, it can lead to a build-up of 'stuck' feelings. This can sometimes feel like a heavy emotional backpack that you carry around and that leaves you feeling low and confused. The thoughts you're carrying can become a blurry mess in your mind.

One way to make things clearer is through journalling. It can help with processing your emotions and letting feelings go by allowing and expressing them. You can say whatever you like on the page without worrying about hurting anyone's feelings. In other words, you can allow yourself 'freedom of the pen' – the freedom to express all your inner thoughts and feelings without censoring or judging them.

Express yourself

Before beginning this exercise, ask yourself if there's a person or situation that feels difficult or challenging in some way. Is there someone you find it difficult to talk to or times when you struggle to express what you really want or need to say?

Take some lined paper and choose a particular person or issue you'd like to resolve. Write this issue at the top of the page. Next spend between 10 and 20 minutes writing down exactly what you think about that person or issue. Just follow the thoughts in your mind and write down exactly what you think, without censoring yourself. You could choose to draw your thoughts instead.

Be the opposite of polite. Write fast, and don't worry about spelling, grammar, punctuation or the neatness of your handwriting. Forget all the standard rules about what's acceptable – use the words you want to use and say exactly what you'd like to say. Remember it's not bad to think these thoughts and expressing them is the first step to being able to let them go.

Clearing your mind

You might find that after doing this for a while, your writing becomes less emotional and more thoughtful. You might now be able to come up with solutions for whatever's been troubling you with a person or situation. Often writing down what you'd really like to say with complete freedom can help clear your mind so that you can think about what you'd actually like to say in real life.

So, for example, imagine you share a bedroom with a sibling (this may be a real-life situation for you), and they're always leaving their stuff around everywhere and it makes you angry. Your first approach might be to shout at them. They might respond angrily when you confront them about it, even though your need for having a tidy space is entirely reasonable. However, taking time to write out your feelings on paper beforehand can be helpful. Afterwards your mind will feel clearer, so you could ask your sibling – in a gentle, reasoned way – if they could tidy up their stuff. They'll be much more likely to agree and you'll get the right result.

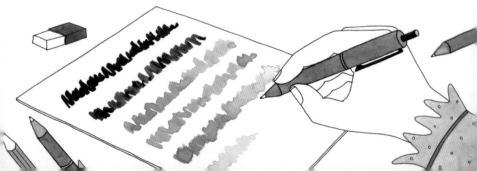

NOT SURE WHERE TO START?

If you're unsure how to embrace the freedom of the pen, here are a few ideas to help you begin journalling:

* Can you remember a situation where you had to bite your tongue and couldn't say what you really wanted to say?
* If you could write a letter (but not send it), to anyone, whether they are dead or alive, what would you say to them?
* Is there someone you'd like to apologise to?
* Is there someone you'd like to forgive?
* Was there a time when someone treated you unfairly?

If any of these writing exercises bring up strong, worrying or overwhelming feelings, always talk to someone you really trust, be that a guardian, doctor, teacher, school counsellor or nurse.

TEARS OF JOY

Bursting into tears when something good happens might seem weird, but leaping (and weeping) for joy is a common and natural response that is expressive and can even be good for your health

Why do people cry when they're happy?

Despite plenty of scientific studies, nobody knows for certain why some cry tears of joy while others stay dry-eyed. It depends upon the individual and how they feel in any given situation. Emotion, which is basically energy in motion, is a powerful response to life's everyday events and happenings. Some people are more sensitive than others and feel things more acutely. As a result, their emotional response can be heightened. Often, they cry easily, sometimes for the slightest thing, and especially at key moments in life. Perhaps you've seen this in people you know, or perhaps this applies to you directly. It's thought that the brain registers intense emotion, whether happy or sad, as simply the same energy and responds the same way through tears. When the nerve receptors are activated, the brain's limbic system, which is connected to emotional responses, stimulates the gland that produces tears. So when an emotional threshold is reached, the tears simply flow. This suggests that it's natural for everyone to express tears of sadness as well as joy. Not everyone finds it easy to cry, or even wants to express themselves, however, especially in public. Some might admit to 'filling up' or feel like they're 'close to tears'; others will choke them back; and more will bawl their eyes out. Whether you let tears of joy flow depends upon the way you feel and your emotions. Everyone is different and either response is fine.

Releasing built-up emotions
Crying when happy can be a form of relief. For example, if you find yourself crying because you achieved the exam results you worked so hard for, the tears could be an expression and a release of the challenges and frustration you experienced while learning and revising. Similarly, if you cry because you've won an award or triumphed at a sporting event, those tears of joy are also likely to be sprinkled with the memory of the pain and hardship you went through to secure your success. It's why you often see professional athletes crying when they've won a medal or achieved their personal best. Some psychologists believe that whatever the reason for crying, allowing the tears to flow helps to restore emotional harmony. It acts as a release valve, letting go of tension and stress you might not even be aware you were carrying. Do you and your friends sometimes laugh so much that you cry? It's thought that vigorous laughing puts pressure on the tear ducts resulting in reflex tears. Those tears rolling down your face are totally natural and even help to keep your eyes healthy.

What to do when you cry tears of joy:

Let them flow. If you feel like crying for joy, allow the tears to flow. Sometimes, your eyes will fill up naturally before you've had a chance to think. Emotions are powerful and you might tremble as you well up with tears, so give yourself time to sit with your feelings. Notice how relaxed and free you are afterwards.

Ignore negative comments. There's no need to be embarrassed. Tears, whether happy or sad, are a healthy response. If someone calls you names for crying or makes you feel uncomfortable, their response says more about them than you. It's quite possible they're bottling up or can't express their own feelings.

Join together. Don't be surprised if your tears of joy make other people cry too. It's quite natural. You'll all end up with tears rolling down your cheeks but this will open the way to smiles, laughter, stronger relationships and deep contentment.

8 WAYS TO GET A GOOD NIGHT'S SLEEP

Sleep is the ultimate mind, body and spirit tonic; it's free and it should come naturally – so why does truly refreshing sleep sometimes seem so tricky to achieve?

Well, like so many things in life, health-giving sleep isn't about quantity, but quality. So here's how to make sure you get some top-notch shut-eye, and that your rest is truly reviving...

1 Think ahead

Resolve to get yourself into a bedtime routine – it's all about convincing your body that the day is drawing to a close and you're ready to wind down, something you should start to do about an hour before bedtime. As far as possible, aim to go to bed at roughly the same time, and with the same rituals before bedtime, every night. Establishing a regular sleep pattern is your aim and far better for you, experts say, than attempting to compensate for irregularity with lie-ins.

2 Plan your last meal of the day

According to dieticians, eating too close to bedtime increases both your blood sugar and insulin levels, which means you'll have a tougher time getting to sleep. Ideally, you should aim for a light dinner that you finish around three hours before you hit the hay. If you do feel peckish before bedtime, a banana makes an excellent choice, as it's a good source of both magnesium and B6, a vitamin that helps the body in creating sleep-promoting serotonin.

3 A place to relax

Make sure your bedroom is as free from clutter as possible, ideally with a soothing decorative scheme – no surprise, perhaps, to learn that red and purple stimulate, while blue relaxes. One survey found that those sleeping in bedrooms decorated in shades of green and yellow were found to be having a good night's sleep, suggesting that there's no need to keep things bland in the bedroom. And what could be cheerier than waking in a room painted a soft, sunshine yellow?

4 Hot or cold?

Are your sheets made from breathable, natural fabrics and is your duvet the right tog for the season?

5 Aim for dark

In the summer months, you may have to work harder to keep light – which stimulates the brain and thus makes sleep less likely – out of your bedroom. You could consider adding a blackout blind or curtains to your window, or for a simpler solution, invest in an eye mask.

6 Bathe your cares away
A relaxing bath before bed is a great way to unwind both mind and body. Make sure the water's not too hot – the aim is to bask, not boil – have a warm towel at the ready, and add a few drops of sleep-inducing lavender or camomile essential oil before you step into the water.

7 Wind down
Just as light is overly stimulating, so, too, is technology. We all know it – yet determining to keep that mobile phone or laptop out of the bedroom can prove tricky. It really does pay to be strong here though, as according to the Sleep Council: 'Blue light emitting from gadgets [mobile phones and computers] stimulates the brain and inhibits melatonin production – the hormone you need to sleep.' Recharge your devices well away from the bedroom and you'll see a surprisingly rapid improvement in the quality of your shut-eye.

8 And if you still can't sleep?
Try to keep your thoughts as positive as you can, however difficult your day may have been, think of three things that have brought you happiness or comfort. Mindfulness is a great way to stop negative thoughts in their tracks. Focus not on the sleep you're not getting, but on the sensation of your body within the bed as it touches the mattress and duvet and the rise and fall of your breathing. Sleep will come!

OUT OF THE DARKNESS

Do you sleep with a night-light because you're afraid of the dark? Being scared of imaginary monsters in the closet or feeling vulnerable in total darkness is a common fear, but there are ways you can try to tackle it

Just about everyone has felt frightened of being in the dark at some stage of their lives. For most people it's something that gradually passes, but for others it can linger longer into adulthood. It can become a problem if the fear gets out of hand, if it recurs or if it's extreme. A severe fear of the dark or night-time is called nyctophobia and it can lead to sleepless nights and anxiety.

Symptoms of nyctophobia include:

* Feeling nervous or anxious in any dark environment.
* Experiencing physical symptoms such as sweating, shaking, increased heart rate and feeling sick.
* Need to sleep with a night-light.
* Reluctance to be out at night or in darkened places.

Cause for concern?

It's not the darkness itself that's frightening – it's the fear of what it might be hiding. When it's dark, the imagination can conjure up a sense of presence, such as those closet monsters, when there's really nothing there. It's natural to be respectful (rather than fearful) of the dark – it's possibly a survival instinct remnant from our cave-living ancestors who really did need to be aware of any danger lurking at night. This may explain the feeling of being more alert and cautious when it's dark because the ancient part of you is hyperaware, looking for the threat of wild animals and enemy attacks. Thankfully, these dangers aren't generally a problem now, so why do some people still feel terrified of the dark?

There may be a variety of reasons, causes or triggers. The fear might stem from an overheard spooky story, watching a scary film or experiencing a recurring nightmare. Although you might not have to fight off wild animals and enemies like your distant ancestors, you might be afraid because you imagine that robbers or kidnappers are lurking in the darkness. Or fear may arise because of an event in your past that made you feel alone, frightened and vulnerable.

FACING YOUR FEAR

Talk about it
Being afraid of the dark, or what it represents, is nothing to be ashamed of. In many instances, people are able to calm their fears by talking about them. Don't suffer in silence. Tell someone you trust, maybe a parent or teacher. It might be helpful to see your doctor if the situation is affecting your sleep or schoolwork.

Challenge the fear
Given that it's often the imagination that's creating the sense of fear, think about changing what it's telling you. After all, if your imagination can create stories that provoke fear, it can change the story so that what you're afraid of disappears into thin air. Think about what scares you in the dark and try to challenge those thoughts. Reassure yourself by saying: 'I'm safe' and 'I feel comfortable here'.

Reframe thoughts
Consider the dark as nurturing, restful, peaceful and safe. See night-time as a chance to get cosy in a soft bed and sleep amazingly well so that you wake feeling energised after having wonderful, happy dreams. By reframing your thoughts in this positive way, you can feel easier and assured about being in a dark place.

Improve self-care
Are you looking after your health and personal wellbeing? Holding in too much stress or carrying around unresolved emotions can make your fear of the dark worse. Be kind to yourself and ask for support where and when it's needed.

Make the dark a friendly space
Create a cosy, tidy bedroom that you see as a safe and comfortable haven where you can relax totally whether the light is on or off. Stick to a regular night-time routine and try to avoid playing video games, looking at a screen or reading scary stories before you go to sleep. If you feel anxious when you're going to sleep, or if you wake up in the middle of the night, breathe calmly and remind yourself that you're in a safe, friendly space.

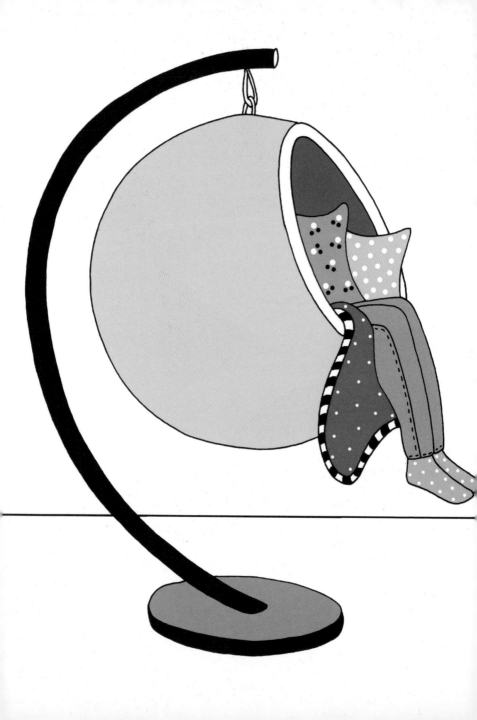

'SOMETIMES IT'S IN THE QUIET THAT WE HEAR THE LOUDEST THINGS'

Anonymous

A PRIVATE HIDEAWAY

Have you ever longed for your own cosy retreat, where you can relax and escape the world for a while? Well, it may be easier than you think to create this special hideaway for yourself. Welcome to the art of cocooning

What is cocooning?
It's basically retreating or taking shelter in a small, comfortable and relaxing space in your room that is cocoon-like – that provides a cosy corner where you can spend a little time whenever you feel the need to think, rest or retreat from the world around you. A cocoon is typically curtained off from everything else in your room to provide a dedicated hideaway where you can snuggle up in your favourite blanket and simply 'be'.

Nature's cocoons
You may have heard of the word cocoon in nature. It's a protective casing, often made of spun silk, which surrounds the pupa of many moths and insect larvae where there is a complete transformation from immature to adult form. In the case of a caterpillar, it can take anything from a few days to a few weeks for it to hatch from its cocoon and emerge as a moth. Butterflies go through a similar process but hatch from a chrysalis, usually made of hardened protein. It's one of nature's spectacular transformations.

Why create a cosy space?

A cocoon offers the perfect space to take refuge and have time to think about who you are and how you relate to the world around you during any intense and confusing times. It also offers a gentle, comforting place where you can retreat when you feel sad, upset or under pressure.

Unlike a caterpillar, you won't be encased in spun silk, but you will have a reassuring corner where you can spend time to reflect. In many ways, your own bedroom-based cocoon can be a transformational space, where you will emerge, like a beautiful butterfly hatching from its chrysalis, with extra clarity, insights and confidence.

But cocooning isn't just to help navigate the frantic, difficult and puzzling times in life. It offers a quiet ambience and an idyllic haven, where you can be yourself, relax deeply and enjoy the simple things that make you feel warm, reassured, happy and content.

Use your cocoon space to:

* Breathe, reflect and meditate.
* Contemplate anything that is bothering you.
* Cry if you feel that you need to.
* Lounge and rest after a busy day.
* Snuggle up and read a book.
* Enjoy a hot chocolate and a biscuit.
* Listen to music.
* Write poetry.
* Doodle in a sketchbook.
* Write in your journal.
* Take a nap.
* Do nothing.
* Dream.

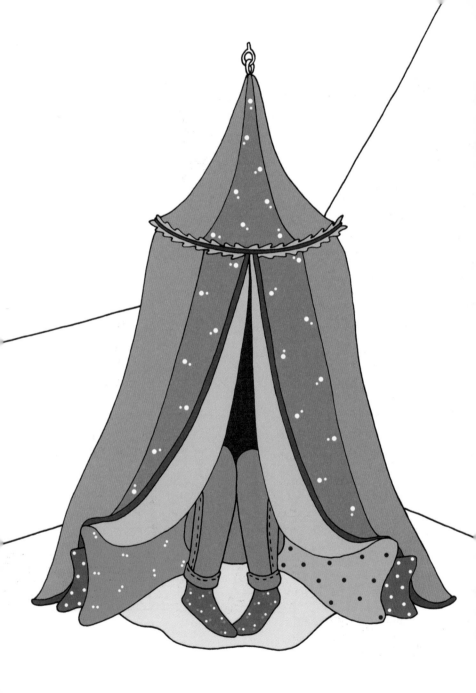

IDEAS FOR YOUR BEDROOM COCOON

Choose your space. It needs to be just big enough for you to lounge in. Perhaps it's an unused corner by your bed or at the side of a cupboard that is out of the way.

Types of cocoon. Take a look on the internet for pictures of cosy bedroom cocoons to give you some ideas and inspiration. A tiny, pop-up tent with a zipped door provides an ideal cocooning space. From hammocks to pods, cocoons come in all shapes and sizes and can be as individual as you are.

Repurpose. You can make your cocoon using furniture and furnishings that you already have. A beanbag or floor cushion might fit in your cosy corner. Then all you need do is cover it with your favourite blanket. If you want to make the space more enclosed and private, see if there's a way to hang a curtain that can be drawn back from the inside.

Make it cosy. Fill the space with extra soft covers, pillows, cushions and a snugly blanket. Focus on making it the ultimate chill-out area that rivals (or is even better than) your bed.

Choose plain fabrics. Avoid using covers or cushions that feature stripes, heavy patterns and busy prints as these can be overstimulating. Plain fabrics in soft, warm colours are easy on the eye and calming for the mind.

Lighting. If you're reading and writing in your cosy space, use a lamp to provide adequate lighting. Otherwise, enjoy relaxing in subdued light. Dark and cosy is best for resting, meditation, sleeping and dreaming.

Clutter-free zone. Avoid decorating the space or filling it with lots of pictures and notes. Keep your cocoon clean, tidy and free of clutter. It will help you to relax more easily and also declutter your mind.

Remember to discuss the idea with your parents before making any changes to your bedroom. They may be able to help with practicalities, such as hanging a curtain, or even offer to buy a few items that will make your cocoon warm, soothing and welcoming. Then all you have to do is sit in your safe haven and enjoy the sensation of calmness and security it provides.

TEEN Breathe

TEEN BREATHE is a trademark of Guild of Master Craftsman Publications Ltd

First published 2022 by Ammonite Press
an imprint of Guild of Master Craftsman Publications Ltd
Castle Place, 166 High Street, Lewes, East Sussex, BN7 1XU, United Kingdom

www.ammonitepress.com
www.teenbreathe.co.uk

Editorial: Susie Duff, Josie Fletcher, Catherine Kielthy, Jane Roe

Publisher: Jonathan Grogan
Designer: Jo Chapman

Words credits: Dawattie Basdeo, Arabella Black, Christine Boggis, Vicky H Bourne,
Karen Bray, Jenny Cockle, Donna Finlay, Anne Guillot, Juliana Kassianos, Anna Lambert,
Nicola Ludlam-Raine, Dr Sarah Maynard, Kate Orson, Natalie Pennicotte-Collier,
Sarah Rodrigues, Sarah Rudell Beach, Carol Anne Strange

Illustrations: Lou Baker Smith, Lucia Calfapietra, Amber Davenport, Varvara Fomina, Beatrix Hatcher,
Claire van Heukelom, Jen Leem-Bruggen, Vanessa Lovegrove, Samantha Nickerson, Nicky Paton,
Irina Perju, Helma Speksnijder, Silvia Stecher, Sara Thielker, Cheryl Thuesday, Rachel Tunstall,
Thomas White, Rose Wong, Shutterstock.com

Cover illustration: Charly Clements

ISBN 978 1 78145 472 5

A catalogue record for this book is available from the British Library

Colour reproduction by GMC Reprographics
Printed and bound in Turkey

AMMONITE
PRESS